Financing Climate Futures

RETHINKING INFRASTRUCTURE

Please cite this publication as:
OECD/The World Bank/UN Environment (2018), *Financing Climate Futures: Rethinking Infrastructure*, OECD Publishing, Paris.
https://doi.org/10.1787/9789264308114-en

ISBN 978-92-64-30810-7 (print)
ISBN 978-92-64-30811-4 (pdf)
ISBN 978-92-64-30910-4 (epub)
ISBN 978-92-64-30911-1 (HMTL)

Photo credits: © jamesteohart / Shutterstock.com

Corrigenda to OECD publications may be found on line at: *www.oecd.org/publishing/corrigenda*.

Foreword

Countries worldwide are recognising the need for immediate action to combat climate change and adapt to its consequences. To date, over 180 countries have ratified the Paris Agreement. However, efforts to achieve global climate goals remain insufficient. Greenhouse gas emissions continue to rise and some governments remain concerned that climate policies could slow economic growth. But this is simply wrong.

As shown in the OECD's 2017 flagship report, Investing in Climate, Investing in Growth — which was supported by the German G20 Presidency — governments can take decisive climate action now that reinforces, rather than undermines, growth prospects. Such action is not only good environmental stewardship, but also sound economic policy since the cost of inaction and delayed efforts will be higher than timely measures taken now. Moreover, climate action presents opportunities to expand and modernise much-needed low-emission, resilient infrastructure, draw on untapped economic potential, drive exciting new technological developments and build more inclusive societies.

Historically, governments have dealt with the climate challenge on the margins, in an incremental and piecemeal fashion. But, as the Inter-Governmental Panel on Climate Change's Special Report on Global Warming of 1.5°C recently reminded us, this will require an urgent and systemic economic transformation. With this transformation in mind, the G20 Hamburg Climate and Energy Action Plan for Growth called on our three organisations – the OECD, UN Environment and the World Bank Group – to work together on approaches to make financial flows consistent with the Paris Agreement goals.

Financing Climate Futures: Rethinking Infrastructure is a product of this work. This report lays out the agenda for integrating climate considerations into all aspects of our societies and setting up the right incentives to better align financial flows by focussing on key transformational action areas: planning, innovation, budgeting, finance, development and cities. Among key steps, governments must plan for long-term climate objectives and disentangle their fiscal reliance on fossil fuels. They should mobilise public and private finance to bridge the infrastructure investment gap in order to meet both development needs and climate objectives. Climate innovations must be developed and widely deployed. And last but not least, action must focus on cities, which are the building blocks of modern societies.

How governments respond today will impact the options available to future generations. The way ahead will not be easy, but the need for action is unquestionable. We call on governments to act on the important recommendations of this report to help them fundamentally shift towards low-emission economies and seize the opportunities presented by the convergence of challenges ahead: social inequalities, sustainable infrastructure deficits and a changing climate.

Angel Gurría	Erik Solheim	Kristalina Georgieva
Secretary-General, OECD	Executive Director, UN Environment	CEO, World Bank Group

Acknowledgements

The *Financing Climate Futures: Rethinking Infrastructure* initiative is a collaborative effort between the Organisation for Economic Co-operation and Development (OECD), the United Nations Environment Programme (UN Environment) and the World Bank Group (WBG). The financial support of the German Federal Ministry for the Environment, Nature Conservation and Nuclear Safety (BMU) is gratefully acknowledged.

The initiative was launched in response to an invitation from the 2017 G20 Hamburg Climate and Energy Action Plan for Growth to "*compile ongoing public and private activities within the G20 for making financial flows consistent with the Paris goals and, building on this, to analyze potential opportunities for strengthening these efforts*".

This report was prepared under the supervision of Anthony Cox and co-ordinated by Virginie Marchal (OECD Environment Directorate). Norbert Gorißen (BMU), John Roome (WBG) and Simon Zadek (UN Environment) provided strategic guidance to the project.

The lead authors are Douglas Herrick (Chapter 2), Kate Kooka (Chapters 4 and 7), Virginie Marchal (Chapters 1 and 5), Michael Mullan (Chapter 2), Edward Perry (Chapter 3) from the OECD Environment Directorate (ENV), and Naeeda Crishna Morgado (Chapter 6) from the OECD Development Co-operation Directorate (DCD).

Particular thanks are expressed to the members of the project core team for their invaluable support, guidance and contributions to the project: Claudia Keller and Till Kötter (BMU), Céline Ramstein (World Bank Group), Zoe Lagarde (OECD) and Felicity Perry (UN Environment Inquiry).

The report benefited from comments and contributions from a number of OECD Directorates: Centre for Entrepreneurship, SMEs and Local Development (CFE); Centre for Tax Policy and Administration (CTP); Directorate for Financial and Enterprise Affairs (DAF); Development Co-operation Directorate (DCD); Economics Department (ECO); Directorate for Employment, Labour and Social Affairs (ELS); Environment Directorate (ENV); Directorate for Public Governance (GOV); Directorate for Science, Technology and Innovation (STI); Trade and Agriculture Directorate (TAD); and the Office of the Secretary General (OSG).

The authors would like to specifically thank the following individuals for their insightful comments and contributions:

UN Environment	Mahenau Agha, Juan Chebly, Iain Henderson, Michael Logan, Marcos Mancini, Olivier Lavagne d'Ortigue, Felicity Perry, Nader Rahman, Simon Zadek
World Bank Group	Carter Brandon, Marianne Fay, Stéphane Hallegatte, Stephen Hammer, Alzbeta Klein, Shagun Mehrotra, Céline Ramstein, John Roome, Julie Rozenberg
BMU	Norbert Gorißen, Claudia Keller, Till Kötter
OECD	CFE: Isabelle Chatry, Dorothée Allain-Dupré, Marissa Plouin, Sena Segbedzi; CTP: Luisa Dressler, Florens Flues, Kurt Van Dender; DAF: Géraldine Ang, Timothy Bishop, Raffaele Della Croce, Joel Paula; DCD: Nicolina Lamhauge, Bérénice Lasfargues, Jens Sedemund, Özlem Taskin; ECO: Andrés Fuentes Hutfilter; ELS: Duncan MacDonald; ENV: Shardul Agrawala, Rodney Boyd, Nils Axel Braathen, Simon Buckle, Lisa Danielson, Antoine Dechezleprêtre, Kathleen Dominique, Kate Eklin, Jane Ellis, Ivan Haščič, Raphaël Jachnik, Katia Karousakis, Britta Labuhn, Mariana Mirabile, Daniel Nachtigall, Mikaëla Rambali, Dirk Röttgers, Isabel Seeger, Robert Youngman; GOV: Juliane Jansen and Paulo Magina; STI: Mario Cervantes, Nick Johnstone, Manuela Vitrella; TAD: Guillaume Gruère

Duncan Cass-Beggs and Julia Staudt provided guidance on the strategic foresight aspects of the project (OSG).

The comments and suggestions from external reviewers are also gratefully acknowledged:

Richard Baron from the 2050 Pathways Platform; Jan Corfee-Morlot from 3CS; Frédéric Asseline from the Asian Development Bank; Mariana Deheza, Damien Navizet, Bertrand Reysset from Agence Française de Développement; Louisa Hall, Robert Moore, Jonny Wyatt from the United Kingdom's Department for Business, Energy and Industrial Strategy; Julia Reinaud from Bill Gates Catalyst 3; Lotte Westermann from the German Federal Ministry for Economic Co-operation and Development (BMZ); Helena Wright from E3G; Sung-Ah Kyun from European Bank for Reconstruction and Development; Sophie Bartosch, Julia Anna Bingler and Lutz Weischer from Germanwatch; Katharina Schneider-Roos from Global Infrastructure Basel; Claudio Alatorre Frenk, Amal-Lee Amin, Marco Buttazzoni, Susana Cardenas, Ivan Corbacho Morales, Maricarmen Esquivel Gallegos, Luz Fernandez García, Giovanni Leo Frisari, Amy Lewis, Mariana Silva Zuniga, Daisy Streatfeild, Adrien Vogt-Schilb and Graham Watkins from the Inter-American Development Bank; Ajay Gambhir and Adam Hawkes from the Grantham Institute Imperial College; Christopher Kaminker from Skandinaviska Enskilda Banken.

The comments and suggestions provided by the following OECD committees are also acknowledged: Environment Policy Committee, Committee on Financial Markets, Development Assistance Committee, Working Party on Climate, Investment and Development, Working Party on Integrating Environmental and Economic Policies, Joint Task Force on Institutional Investors and Long-Term Financing, and the DAC Network on Environment and Development Co-operation.

The three organisations are grateful to the participants of the two workshops that were organised as part of the initiative:

- *"Financing infrastructure for a sustainable future"*, Washington DC, 25-26 April 2018.
- *"Aligning financial flows with low-emission, resilient infrastructure"*, Paris, 28-29 June 2018.

The report also benefited from other outputs developed as part of the initiative:

- *Shifting the Lens*, a publication led by UN Environment that explores the benefit of scenarios and foresight approaches in informing climate policies, infrastructure investments and financing decisions today to trigger the transformation needed.
- A series of forthcoming case studies on specific jurisdictions, technologies or actors that could play an important role in the transition:
  - *Achieving clean energy access in sub-Saharan Africa*, Corfee-Morlot, J., P. Parks, J. Ogunleye and F. Ayeni.
  - *Blockchain, infrastructure and the low-emission transition*, OECD.
  - *Digital finance and citizen action in financing the future of climate-smart infrastructure*, UN Environment.
  - *Emerging strategies for decarbonising energy-intensive industries*, Oluleye, G., N. Shah, A.D. Hawkes, Imperial College London Consultants.
  - *Financing resilient urban infrastructure: Lessons from World Bank and global experience*, The World Bank Group.
  - *Mobilising commercial capital for sustainable infrastructure: Insights from national development banks in Brazil and South Africa*, OECD.
  - *Financing climate objectives in cities and regions to deliver sustainable and inclusive growth*, OECD.

The report was prepared for publication under the supervision of Elizabeth Del Bourgo from the OECD Environment Directorate, with editorial work being undertaken by Fiona Hinchcliffe. Thank you to OECD Public Affairs and Communication Directorate colleagues Janine Treves for editorial and content support, and Catherine Bremer for media relation support. Christina Theophilidou of the OECD Environment Directorate provided editorial and secretarial support to the project, and production support was provided by Jessica Li and Stéphanie Simonin-Edwards.

Table of contents

Tables

Figures

Boxes

Acronyms and abbreviations

ADB	Asian Development Bank
AfDB	African Development Bank
AFD	*Agence Française de Développement* (French development agency)
AFOLU	Agriculture, Forestry and Other Land-Use
APEC	Asia-Pacific Economic Co-operation
B2B	Business-to-business
BMU	German Federal Ministry of the Environment, Nature Conservation and Nuclear Safety
BNDES	*Banco Nacional de Desenvolvimento Econômico e Social* (Brazilian development bank)
BRI	Belt and Road Initiative
BRICS	Brazil, Russia, India, China, South Africa
CBA	Cost-benefit analysis
CDB	China Development Bank
CDC	UK Commonwealth Development Corporation
CGC	Coalition for Green Capital
CO_2	Carbon dioxide
CO_2e	Carbon dioxide equivalent
DAC	OECD Development Assistance Committee
DBSA	Development Bank of Southern Africa
DDPP	Deep Decarbonisation Pathways Platform
DFI	Development Finance Institution
FSB	Financial Stability Board
EBRD	European Bank for Reconstruction and Development
EIA	U.S. Energy Information Administration
EIB	European Investment Bank
EPG	The G20 Eminent Persons Group on Global Financial Governance
ESG	Environmental, Social and Governance
EU	European Union
FAO	Food and Agriculture Organization of the United Nations
G7	Group of 7: Canada, France, Germany, Italy, Japan, the United States and the United Kingdom

G20	Group of 20: Argentina, Australia, Brazil, Canada, the People's Republic of China, France, Germany, India, Indonesia, Italy, Japan, Republic of Korea, Mexico, Russia, Saudi Arabia, South Africa, Turkey, the United Kingdom, the United States and the European Union
GCF	Green Climate Fund
GDP	Gross Domestic Product
GEF	Global Environment Facility
GHG	Greenhouse gas
GIH	Global Infrastructure Hub
GPIF	Japan's Government Pension Investment Fund
HLEG	High-Level Expert Group
IDB	Inter-American Development Bank
IDDRI	*Institut du Développement Durable et des Relations Internationales* (French sustainable development and international relations think tank)
IDFC	International Development Finance Club
IEA	International Energy Agency
IFC	International Finance Corporation
IFI	International Financial Institutions
IoT	Internet of Things
IPCC	Intergovernmental Panel on Climate Change
ITF	International Transport Forum
KfW	*Kreditanstalt für Wiederaufbau* (German development bank)
MDB	Multilateral Development Bank
MEAT	Most Economically Advantageous Tender
NDB	National Development Bank
NDC	Nationally Determined Contribution
ODA	Official Development Assistance
ODF	Official Development Finance
PAYG	Pay-As-You-Go
PG&E	Pacific Gas and Electricity
PINES	*Proyectos estratégicos de interés nacional* (Colombia's Strategic Projects of National Interest)
PPP	Public Private Partnership
PRI	UN Principles of Responsible Investment
R&D	Research and Development
REDD+	Reducing Emissions from Deforestation and forest Degradation, plus the sustainable management of forests, and the conservation and enhancement of forest carbon stocks
SCC	Social cost of carbon
SDG(s)	Sustainable Development Goal(s)

SDSN	Sustainable Development Solutions Network
SEforAll	Sustainable Energy for All
SHS	Solar Household System
SIF	Sustainable Insurance Forum
SME	Small and Medium Sized Enterprise
SOE	State-Owned Enterprise
SWF	Sovereign Wealth Fund
TCFD	Task Force on Climate-related Financial Risk Disclosure
TSKB	*Türkiye Sınai Kalkınma Bankası* (Industrial Development Bank of Turkey)
UNFCCC	United Nations Framework Convention on Climate Change
UN	United Nations
UNDESA	United Nations Department of Economic and Social Affairs
UNEP	UN Environment (United Nations Environment Programme)
WBG	World Bank Group

Financing Climate Futures
Rethinking Infrastructure
© OECD/The World Bank/UN Environment, 2018

Executive summary

Infrastructure sits at the very centre of development pathways and underpins economic growth, productivity and well-being. Yet infrastructure has suffered from chronic underinvestment for decades, in both developed and developing economies. The OECD estimates that USD 6.9 trillion a year is required up to 2030 to meet climate and development objectives. Furthermore, current energy, transport, building and water infrastructure make up more than 60% of global greenhouse gas emissions. An unprecedented transformation of existing infrastructure systems is needed to achieve the world's climate and development objectives.

Aligning financial flows with low-emission, resilient development pathways is now more critical than ever to meet the goals of the Paris Agreement and deliver on the 2030 Agenda for Sustainable Development. Today there is a unique opportunity to develop infrastructure systems that deliver better services while protecting the environment. Harnessing the benefits of rapidly emerging technologies, new business models and financial innovations will be key in opening new pathways to low-emission, resilient futures.

Mobilising public and private resources across the financial spectrum is an essential part of generating the trillions of dollars needed for sustainable infrastructure. Public finance institutions, banks, institutional investors, corporations and capital markets all have a crucial role to play, both in their own right and as part of the broader financial ecosystem.

Governments need to set the right incentives to mobilise finance away from emissions-intensive projects, and provide investment and climate policy frameworks that support the rapid and radical transformations required. While there has been some progress, current policies continue to foster an incremental approach to climate. Existing policy frameworks, government revenues and economic interests continue to be entangled in fossil fuels and emissions-intensive activities. Deeper efforts are needed to drive systemic change, overcome institutional inertia and break away from the vested interests that are often barriers to low-emission, resilient development.

Enhanced international co-operation, through the Paris Agreement or fora such as the G7 and the G20, is an essential part of the transformation. The international community has increasingly recognised the need for such transformation: almost all G20 countries confirmed their willingness to embark on a global energy transition in line with climate and development goals in the 2017 G20 Hamburg Climate and Energy Action Plan for Growth. There is also growing awareness that the push for greater climate action must be accompanied by a just and inclusive transition to address inequalities and provide equal opportunities for all parts of society. Governments need to ensure that the transition benefits everyone and does not disproportionately affect the poor and most vulnerable.

This report lays out an agenda to enable societies around the world to undertake the kind of systemic actions that the transformation towards a low-emission, resilient future will require. It highlights 6 transformative areas and 20 actions that are key to aligning financial flows with climate and development goals in the areas of planning, innovation, public budgeting, financial systems, development finance and cities.

- **Plan infrastructure for a low-emission and resilient future**, by rethinking planning at all levels of governments to align current infrastructure project plans with long-term climate and development objectives, avoid carbon lock-in and make resilience the norm in infrastructure decisions.
- **Unleash innovation to accelerate the transition,** by deploying targeted innovation policies and accelerating the deployment of existing technologies, business models and services, swiftly moving the next generation of solutions from the lab to the market, and promoting international technology diffusion to make sure innovation benefits all.
- **Ensure fiscal sustainability for a low-emission, resilient future**, by diversifying sources of government revenue to reduce carbon entanglement, aligning fiscal and budgetary incentives with climate objectives and harnessing the power of public procurement and public institutions' spending while ensuring an inclusive transition along the way.
- **Reset the financial system in line with long-term climate risks and opportunities**, by fixing biased incentives, capability gaps and inadequate climate risk disclosure and pricing that are hindering the allocation of finance to low-emission, resilient infrastructure.
- **Rethink development finance for climate,** by ensuring that development finance institutions have the resources, mandates and incentives to deliver transformative climate action, attract new investors and sources of finance by using concessional finance strategically, and help countries advance their climate agendas and build enabling environments and "climate markets".
- **Empower city governments to build low-emission and resilient urban societies**, by developing capacity to more effectively plan and finance the right infrastructure, aligning national and local fiscal regulations with investment needs, and building climate-related and project finance capacity at the city level.

Delivering on the transformation will be challenging. While there is encouraging momentum, governments must continue to drive systemic changes to ensure that financial flows are well aligned with the infrastructure needed for low-emission, resilient pathways to the future. Moving towards a more transformative agenda will help governments deliver sustainable, balanced and inclusive growth and improve well-being within and across societies.

Financing Climate Futures
Rethinking Infrastructure

Chapter 1

Climate, infrastructure and finance: An agenda for transformation

Aligning financial flows with low-emission, resilient infrastructure is essential to deliver climate and development objectives. Infrastructure underpins economic growth, productivity and well-being. A fundamental transformation of existing infrastructure systems is needed to meet the scale and urgency of climate action. Getting investment and climate policy right is a necessary condition of success, but it is not enough. Existing policy frameworks, institutions and economic incentives encourage incremental changes. Only systemic change will disrupt institutional inertia and vested interests that slow the pace of change in climate and development policy. This chapter contains an extended synthesis of the report, laying out the agenda for governments to move away from incremental progress on climate change to deliver the transformation needed. It highlights why and how action across six transformative areas – planning, innovation, public budgeting, financial systems, development finance and cities – can help align financial flows with climate and development goals.

Key messages

Infrastructure sits at the very centre of climate and development pathways. It underpins the development of societies, economic growth, productivity and well-being. Yet current energy, transport, buildings and water infrastructure make up more than 60% of greenhouse gas emissions, and infrastructure worldwide has suffered from chronic underinvestment for decades. A fundamental transformation of existing infrastructure systems is needed to meet the scale and the urgency of climate action.

Aligning public and private investments in low-emission and resilient infrastructure has now become critical to increase resilience, avoid further emissions lock-in, and deliver on climate and the Sustainable Development Goals. Getting investment and climate policy right is a necessary condition of success in meeting the climate challenge, but it is not enough. Existing policy frameworks, institutions and economic incentives encourage incremental changes when a rapid transformation is needed. Only systemic change will disrupt the roots of institutional inertia and vested interests that serve to frustrate and slow the pace of change in climate and development policy.

This report lays out the agenda for a low-emission, resilient transformation that governments, the private sector and civil society need to focus on in order to move beyond an incremental approach to the climate challenge and pursue a truly transformative agenda. It requires action across six areas: planning, innovation, budgeting, financial systems, development and cities, and a whole-of-government, whole-of-society approach to the climate challenge.

1.1. A fundamental transformation of existing infrastructure systems is needed

The climate challenge calls for rapid and far-reaching transformations in energy, land-use, transport and urban systems

A pathway compatible with the objective of the Paris Agreement to limit global temperature increase to well-below 2°C and towards 1.5°C above pre-industrial levels requires a radical change to infrastructure, technologies and behaviours. Significant greenhouse gas emissions are embedded in the vast majority of human activities and preferences. The world's energy, transport, buildings and water systems emit more than 60% of current greenhouse gases. Emissions are increasing as a result of several trends: an increased appetite for mobility and ownership of individual cars; a growing population that is expected to move towards meat-intensive food diets, which puts more pressure on agricultural productivity; use of cement and aluminium in house construction; and increasing reliance on heating and cooling systems.

The urgency and scale of the infrastructure challenge was starkly laid out in the Intergovernmental Panel on Climate Change (IPCC)'s special report on the impacts of global warming of 1.5°C above pre-industrial levels (IPCC, 2018[1]). To limit warming to 1.5°C, CO_2 emissions must fall by about 45% by 2030 compared to 2010 levels, and would need to reach net-zero around 2050. The report concludes that "rapid and far-reaching transitions in energy, land, urban and infrastructure (including transport and buildings) and industrial systems" are required in order to limit global warming to 1.5°C. It highlights the need for an unprecedented transition across these systems, and a significant increase in investments in mitigation options: Annual investment in low-carbon energy and energy efficiency would need to increase by a factor of five by 2050.

While there are many different pathways to achieve carbon neutrality, all require action across the following systems (IPCC, 2018[1]):

- **Energy**. Today's energy systems rely heavily on centralised power generation based on fossil fuels. Tomorrow's energy systems will need to see a substantial reduction in demand through energy efficiency, a decline in the carbon intensity of electricity to zero by mid-century, and an increase in electrification of energy uses. In a pathway consistent with 1.5°C warming, renewables supply 70-85% of the electricity in 2050, while coal disappears from the electricity mix by 2050 (IPCC, 2018[1]).
- **Land use**. A sustainable intensification of land-use practices, enhanced agricultural productivity and potentially a change in dietary preferences will be necessary in order to meet the goals of poverty reduction, access to food, biodiversity conservation, and climate and development objectives. Changes in urban planning are also essential. Limiting urban sprawl is particularly important in the context of cities in developing countries, which are projected to grow rapidly in the coming decades.
- **Heavy industries**. Cement, aluminium, chemicals and steel are essential to the built environment and to manufacturing, and will remain so for decades to come. Yet their production is extremely energy- and emissions-intensive. A significant transformation of such energy-intensive industries is needed, going beyond energy efficiency measures to more innovative business models and technologies.
- **Transport and buildings**. Current transport systems rely largely on fossil fuels and impose a very high environmental cost (air pollution, noise and congestion). Improving the energy efficiency of transport and buildings is a key step, with more efficient vehicles or appliances, insulation of existing buildings and electrification of vehicles. Demand measures are also required to reduce the need for mobility through more efficient public transport and a better integration of land-use planning and transport policies.

Getting the infrastructure investment right in these systems is one of the key success factors to achieving the goals of the Paris Agreement and delivering on development and growth objectives. Given its long life span, infrastructure could also lock in emissions-intensive behaviours for decades to come. The new demand for infrastructure in a low-emission world is an opportunity for emerging and developing countries to "leapfrog" the emissions-intensive, fossil-fuel oriented infrastructure systems of the past (New Climate Economy, 2016[2]). Better infrastructure is also needed to enhance the resilience of economic systems, social structures and communities as a certain amount of climate change is already locked into the system. There is a unique opportunity in the coming years to develop infrastructure systems that deliver better services while protecting the environment.

Greater infrastructure investment is required to support development

Infrastructure worldwide has suffered from chronic underinvestment for decades, leading to a lack of infrastructure services. Climate-related requirements regarding infrastructure quality come on top of this pre-existing infrastructure investment gap. The urgent need to address this issue presents a unique opportunity in the coming years to move the climate and development agendas forward and develop infrastructure systems that deliver better services while also achieving climate and development goals. Which infrastructure projects receive financing will shape not only development patterns but will also determine future emissions pathways. Recent OECD estimates indicate that around USD 6.3 trillion of infrastructure investment is needed each year to 2030 to meet the Sustainable Development Goals (SDGs), increasing to USD 6.9 trillion a year over the same period to make this investment compatible with the goals of the Paris Agreement (OECD, 2017[3]). The current spending on infrastructure is between USD 3.4-4.4 trillion, depending on the measurement metrics used.

In developing economies, significant levels of investment are needed to upgrade current infrastructure systems and to develop new infrastructure projects to deliver on the Sustainable Development Goals (SDGs). A decisive transition towards a low-emission, resilient future can serve to safeguard the significant gains made in improving human development in past decades.

The latest progress report by the UN Secretary General on the achievement of the SDGs shows that global poverty[1] has declined rapidly, dropping to one-third of 1990 levels in 2013, but that 783 million people still lived in poverty in 2013 (UN Economic and Social Council, 2018[4]). But poorer populations and communities are often the most vulnerable to the impacts of a changing climate and without decisive action, increasing climate impacts could drive more than 100 million people into poverty by 2030 (Hallegatte et al., 2016[5]). Solving the refugee crisis has been a defining development issue for both developed and developing countries in recent years, and climate change could exacerbate this further. A World Bank Group analysis shows that climate change could induce over 143 million people from three regions – sub-Saharan Africa, South Asia, and Latin America – to migrate out of their own countries (Rigaud et al., 2018[6]).

The infrastructure gap is no less a serious concern for developed economies. These economies are at a different stage of the infrastructure cycle, but significant levels of infrastructure investment are needed to maintain and upgrade ageing infrastructure. Public investment in advanced G20 economies fell from 5% of GDP in the late 1960s to 3% in the mid-2000s (OECD, 2017[3]). Despite increased infrastructure investment following the recent financial crisis, spending remains at a historic low, resulting in ageing and poorly maintained infrastructure stock in many developed economies.

A greater role for natural infrastructure and the land-use sectors

Natural infrastructure has a significant role to play in filling the infrastructure gap, both in terms of increasing the efficiency of delivering essential ecosystem-based services and of reducing the cost of infrastructure. Healthy, functional ecosystems can provide services that complement or provide a cost-effective alternative to those provided by grey (civil-engineered) infrastructure. Restoring wetlands and protecting watersheds, for example, can help filter water and regulate water flow, ensuring continued access to clean water and protecting communities and infrastructure from flooding (see Chapter 2).

Similarly, land-use sectors hold considerable potential to deliver mitigation and adaptation benefits, and they are also highly sensitive to climate change. Increasing temperatures are projected to affect – and in some cases have already affected – the ability of land to store carbon, the productivity of land (particularly due to changes in precipitation levels) and the resilience of ecosystems. Measures are needed to enhance the resilience of ecosystems and help adapt agriculture to climate change (e.g. climate-resilient crop varieties, advanced irrigation technologies).

Rapid changes in technologies and business models lie ahead

Rapid technological, economic and societal changes are generating high uncertainty around a number of variables that could impact climate change mitigation and adaptation efforts in the coming decades. These potential changes and disruptions could radically change the demand for infrastructure, creating new opportunities and challenges for achieving climate goals that must be taken into account in making infrastructure investment decisions today.

Such disruptive technologies include:

- Enabling technologies, such as the Internet of Things (IoT), blockchain, artificial intelligence, machine learning, 3D printing and large powerful batteries;
- Sector-specific technologies, such as autonomous vehicles and electric vehicles;
- Business models that change the demand for infrastructure supply, such as sharing economy and circular economy models; and
- Digital finance instruments such as pay-as-you-go systems that create new opportunities for financing infrastructure services and influencing behaviours.

Innovation in technologies, business models and financing tools creates new opportunities for climate and development. Sharing economy business models could reduce the demand for mobility and housing infrastructure. Disruptive technologies and business models could also reduce oil demand by a third compared to a business-as-usual scenario (Thomä, Dupré and Fulton, 2018[7]).

Advances in digitalisation present transformative opportunities to decarbonise and decentralise energy systems: Smart charging technologies for electric vehicles could help address intermittency in renewable energy supply, which could reduce infrastructure investment needs by between USD 100 billion and USD 280 billion in the next two decades. Smart demand response could contribute a further USD 270 billion to infrastructure investment savings (IEA, 2017[8]). Digital finance is also transforming the infrastructure-investment value chain, enabling citizens to participate more directly in investments and unlocking new sources of finance for infrastructure (see Chapter 3).

The importance of the disruption created by those innovations lies not only in the existence or availability of such technologies or business models, but also in the ability for developed and developing countries alike to widely adopt and diffuse such innovations and practices. This is highly dependent on the ability of policy makers, regulators and planning authorities to create appropriate enabling policy and regulatory frameworks, as well as incentive structures that are conducive to the emergence of new technologies. These technologies also need to be widely available in order to ensure that they do not in turn exacerbate inequalities between and within societies (see Chapter 3).

1.2. Moving beyond an incremental policy approach to climate, infrastructure and finance

Current policies tend to foster an incremental approach towards climate goals

While there is clearly some progress in developing and implementing policies in support of sustainable infrastructure, it has proven to be challenging to move beyond relatively marginal or incremental changes to policies and behaviours. On the positive side, more countries are implementing carbon pricing policies and instruments, removing fossil fuel subsidies, carrying out regulatory interventions for energy efficiency and providing targeted support to low-emission innovation. The number of carbon-pricing initiatives has more than tripled in the last 10 years at the national and subnational level (World Bank and Ecofys, 2018[9]). Countries' efforts in supporting low-emission technologies resulted in a significant decrease of the cost of low-emission technologies, which are increasingly competitive with emissions-intensive alternatives, even in the absence of policy support. Global investments in renewable electricity technologies have grown from USD 226 billion in 2000 to USD 298 billion in 2017, and are now more than double the annual investments in fossil fuel generation (IEA, 2018[10]) (see Chapter 4).

There is also momentum for change in the financial system. Public and private financial actors are increasingly aware of the role that finance can play in delivering on sustainable development and climate goals, beyond a relatively narrow focus on corporate social responsibility. Since 2013, the number of subnational and national policy and regulatory measures to promote sustainable finance doubled; notable examples include China's 2016 "Guidelines for Establishing a Green Financial System" and the 2018 European Commission Action Plan on Financing Sustainable Growth (European Commission, 2018[11]).

At the international level, the number of initiatives focusing on the incorporation of sustainability into the international financial rules quadrupled since 2013 (UNEP Inquiry, 2018[12]). There are encouraging developments in the G20 on sustainable infrastructure, with work on new metrics, definitions, standards and financial products as part of the Sustainable Finance Study Group and the Sustainable Insurance Forum. The report of the Financial Stability Board's Task Force on Climate-related Financial Risk Disclosure (TCFD) has been a game-changer in improved awareness, risk analysis and reporting in the corporate sector (TCFD, 2017[13]) (see Chapter 5).

Yet progress to date remains incremental across the board – on emissions reductions, policy ambitions and capital re-allocation. Since 1990, world GDP has more than doubled while CO_2 emissions from fossil fuels increased by 60% (OECD, 2017[3]). Climate action planned or currently underway, while heading in the right direction, has proven insufficient to deliver the transition required. While the rate of emissions growth slowed considerably and energy emissions were flat for three years up until 2016, global emissions rose again in 2017, driven in particular by strong economic growth and a slowdown in energy efficiency improvement (IEA, 2018[14]). Far greater efforts are needed to both reverse that trend, bring about an early global peaking of CO_2 emissions and avoid lock-in to emissions-intensive development pathways.

The combined emissions abatement that governments have pledged to achieve by 2030 in the latest nationally determined contributions (NDCs) still lead to emission levels incompatible with the goals of the Paris Agreement. Even if all abatement targets in the 2030 NDCs were met, global emissions would still be off track by an amount equal to between a fifth and a quarter of total annual emissions globally (UNEP, 2017[15]). To get on a least cost pathway compatible with a well-below 2°C target, governments would need to approximately triple current commitments to emissions reductions in their 2030 Nationally Determined Contributions (NDCs). Continuing with business-as-usual, countries' emissions will already have surpassed levels consistent with 1.5°C by 2030 and consume about 80% of the remaining carbon budget consistent with 2°C (UNEP, 2017[15]).

Progress in developing the necessary policy frameworks is also insufficient. Carbon pricing policies are not ambitious enough. Close to half of emissions are not priced at all: Only 12% of carbon emissions are priced at EUR 30 per tonne of CO_2 or higher, a low-end estimate of the damage that carbon emissions cause and close to half of emissions are not priced at all (OECD, 2018[16]). This figure is even higher in sectors such as agriculture and industry. More efforts are needed to remove fossil fuel subsidies, as estimates of support to fossil fuels range between USD 373 billion and USD 617 billion over the period 2010-2015[2] (OECD, 2018[17]).

The limited existing evidence suggests that progress on capital reallocation and in greening the financial system remains marginal. Low-emission infrastructure investment remains less than 1% of the overall portfolios of institutional investors (G20 Green Finance Study Group, 2016[18]). Current green bonds have been estimated to exceed USD 1 trillion, yet this new asset class makes up less than 1% of the global USD 100 trillion bond market.

In the energy sector, infrastructure investment patterns fail to demonstrate the shift of capital required for the low-emission transition (see Figure 1.1). In 2017, investments in infrastructure for electricity generation from renewable sources were comparable to investments in electricity networks and more than double those of fossil fuel-based electricity generation. But investments in extraction and transport of fossil fuels, oil refining and construction of fossil fuels power plants still represented 57.1% of global investment in energy supply in 2017 (IEA, 2018[10]).

Figure 1.1. **Global energy investments, 2017**

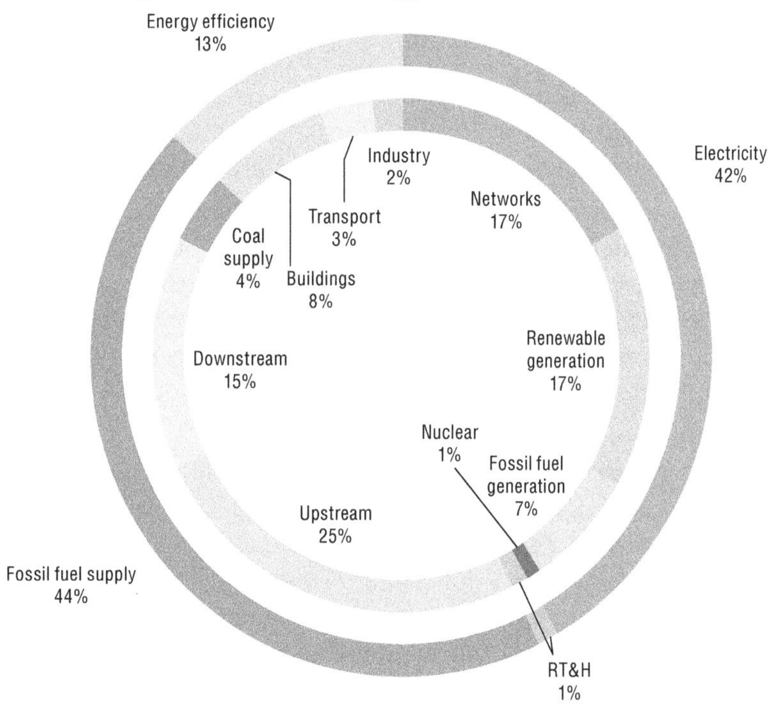

Notes: RT&H = Renewable Transport & Heating. Networks includes battery storage.
Source: IEA (2018[10]), *World Energy Investment 2018*, International Energy Agency, Paris, *https://www.iea.org/wei2018/*

StatLink *https://doi.org/10.1787/888933856359*

Accelerating efforts to re-direct finance flows has now become critical

Addressing the sustainable infrastructure challenge requires mobilising actors across the financial spectrum, from public finance institutions to banks, institutional investors, corporations and capital markets. The importance of finance in climate action is recognised in Article 2.1c of the Paris Agreement, which calls for "making finance flows consistent with a pathway towards low greenhouse gas emissions and climate-resilient development" (UNFCCC, 2015[20]).

The scale of this transformation is such that government budgets are insufficient to generate the trillions of dollars required and must be supplemented by private resources. Mobilising private investment towards the transition is therefore essential. While private finance must play an expanded role, it will be limited to infrastructure projects with clear revenue streams. The public sector will need to continue to support infrastructure, especially in developing countries.

Low-emission, resilient infrastructure investment faces different types of barriers in attracting financing. In addition to the broad barriers linked to attracting financing in long-term infrastructure, particularly in developing countries, there are specific barriers to investments in low-emission infrastructure. These include higher upfront costs, higher technology risks, higher regulatory risks as returns often rely on government subsidies and policies and different risk perceptions. These barriers result in a high degree of status quo bias in the financial system.

Overcoming barriers to mobilise private sector investment at scale requires action across three core areas in a co-ordinated way (Fay et al., 2015[21]). First, governments should make greater efforts to improve the overall business environment and the investment climate. This means, amongst other things, implementing clear and predictable regulations, enforcing property rights and the rule of law, growing local financial markets, and developing options to mitigate regulatory, corruption and currency risks. In the case of developing countries, this imperative needs to be balanced with the political and economic reality of the institutional environment and the urgency of action that needs to happen despite weak investment conditions and immature capital markets in many of these countries.

Second, developing a strong and stable climate policy framework to orient the economy away from emissions-intensive activities is essential to level the playing field with low-emission alternatives. Core climate policies are an essential component of such a framework, including measures such as a robust and credible price on emissions, regulatory measures when pricing is not efficient or too low, fossil fuel subsidy reform and specific measures to bring low-emission technologies to commercialisation.

Third, aligning the overall policy framework with climate goals is essential (OECD, 2015[22]). For instance, a number of obstacles embedded in current financial systems and regulations that are hindering the allocation of finance to long-term low-emission infrastructure investments need to be addressed. Such barriers range from the lack of definitions, information, data and capacities on low-emission, resilient infrastructure investment, to the governance of financial institutions and the financial system as a whole, including financial incentives across the system that favour short-termism (UNEP Inquiry, 2015[23]; Maimbo et al., 2017[24]).

Systemic change is needed to address the underlying problems of institutional inertia and vested interests

Levelling the playing field and adjusting the risk-return profile of low-emission investments is an important element to re-orient flows to low-emission infrastructure, but it is not enough. Infrastructure investment decisions are taking place in an increasingly complex environment. Rapid technological, economic and societal changes are generating uncertainty around a number of variables that could affect the nature of demand for future infrastructure, as well as altering the climate change mitigation and adaptation challenges in coming decades (UN Environment, 2018[25]).

The rapid and disruptive advances in technologies also underscore the significant range and scale of uncertainties confronting decision makers today as they grapple with issues that will have long-term impacts on emissions pathways and resilience. Given the likely breadth and depth of change that societies are facing, the world in 2050 is likely to look significantly different in many ways to the world today. Looking ahead using existing models could hamper decision making in an increasingly non-linear world. Tools such as strategic foresight can serve to highlight the "critical uncertainties" that today's decision makers need to be aware of in order to ensure that current institutional, planning and infrastructure systems can adequately and robustly take such uncertainties into account (see Box 1.1).

Our current institutional settings, processes and institutions are simply not fit to achieve the transformation needed. Governments need to move away from a sectoral approach to infrastructure planning and financing, and move towards a more systemic, forward-looking and whole-of-government approach to infrastructure decisions. Current infrastructure planning practices, decision-making processes and institutional settings inherited from the last century reflect a status quo based on conventional practices and a continued "silo mentality". Innovation and transformation depend on the engagement of parts of governments that so far have not been sufficiently mobilised in the development of climate response strategies, notably ministries of finance, planning and economy, to ensure a good connection between the real economy and the financial system. New approaches to planning need to complement traditional approaches. Foresight methodology provides a complementary perspective by constructing multiple plausible futures to inform decision making under uncertainty (see Chapter 2).

Overcoming this institutional inertia means addressing a series of barriers inherent to our processes, practices and institutions that are preventing more ambitious climate action, including:

- Behavioural and data biases that encourage choices based on conventional practices rather than forward-looking potential;
- Misaligned incentives and capacity gaps along the investment value chain, from procurement to investment decisions; and
- Political economy factors, such as employment in the fossil fuel industry, government rents from fossil fuel-based activities, short time horizons, as well as citizens and incumbent market interests (Röttgers and Anderson, 2018[26]; Maimbo et al., 2017[24])

A just and inclusive transition is essential for a transformative agenda

The push for greater climate action is accompanied by a need for policies that address inequalities and provide the same opportunities for all. Across the OECD, the top 10% of the income distribution earn around 10 times more than the bottom 10%, up from just 7 times more 30 years ago. Climate change threatens to increase the effects of structural inequalities worldwide. Even though wealthier populations may have more assets at risk of climate change impacts, disadvantaged populations tend to be more vulnerable and suffer disproportionately from a changing climate (UNDESA, 2015[27]; Hallegatte et al., 2016[5]). This is because they often live in areas more exposed to climate risks with poor quality housing that is not equipped to resist extreme weather events or lack access to air conditioning in the case of heat waves, for example. They may also be less equipped to recover from a disaster, with reduced access to safety nets like unemployment or insurance systems.

Box 1.1. **Shifting the Lens**

As a component of the Financing Climate Futures initiative, the *Shifting the Lens* report has explored how foresight methodologies and scenario development can better inform infrastructure investment decisions today in order to align financial flows with a low-emission, resilient future (see Figure 1.2).

Figure 1.2. **Foresight and scenario development**

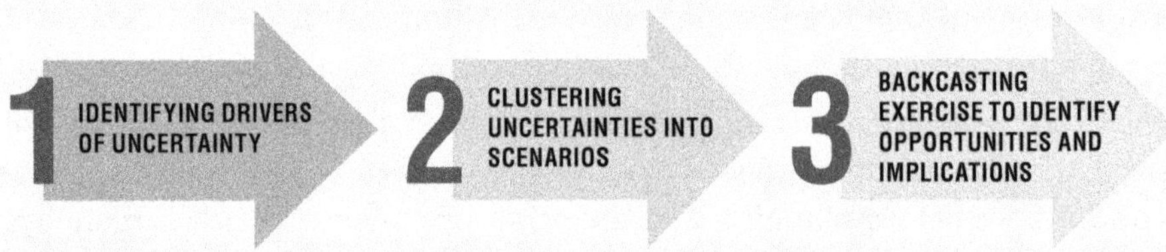

In general, infrastructure decisions today do not take adequate account of critical socioeconomic and technological uncertainties that will shape future infrastructure supply and demand. Scenarios can improve current infrastructure decisions by examining them against an "organised" set of uncertain, plausible futures. Through such a lens, distortions in decision making can be revealed, and adjustments made. Such distortions may arise from a combination of biases embedded in habits and norms, prevalent incentives, incumbent interests, or a lack of competencies.

Shifting the Lens has used a simple analytic framework to identify a number of critical uncertainties that affect future infrastructure demand and supply (see Figure 1.3)

Figure 1.3. **Four-tier analytic framework**

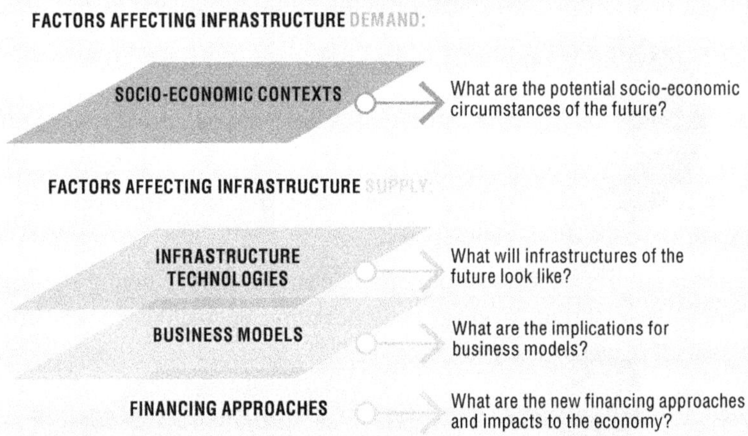

Building on this framework, a number of critical uncertainties have been identified that influence the selection, design, procurement, deployment and related financing decisions regarding low-emission, resilient infrastructure. These include: (1) climate change itself; (2) shifts in the economic and geopolitical features of globalisation; (3) the technological intensification of infrastructure; (4) new economic, business and financing models such as the shared and circular economy; (5) new forms of citizen engagement; (6) changes to the financial system; and (7) economic downturns and external shocks.

To highlight the central role of uncertainty in investment decisions, scenarios were developed to identify clusters of the selected critical uncertainties. It should be emphasised that the scenarios are neither prescriptive nor are they projections. Furthermore, they do not necessarily reflect the views of the organisations involved in preparing this report. They were developed by drawing on the outcomes of dialogue with key stakeholders through workshops and interviews.

Box 1.1. **Shifting the Lens** *(cont.)*

Each scenario has a core characterisation (see Figure 1.4) and seeks to highlight how combinations of critical uncertainties can lead to quite different directions and sensitivities for today's decision makers. Adequate investment in climate-compatible infrastructure is required under all scenarios. These scenarios are intended to highlight possible aspects of a future within which climate goals need to be attained, not to predict or indicate any preference of one over other scenarios. Scenarios therefore help to "stress test" today's policies, financing decisions and civil actions.

Figure 1.4. **Scenarios**

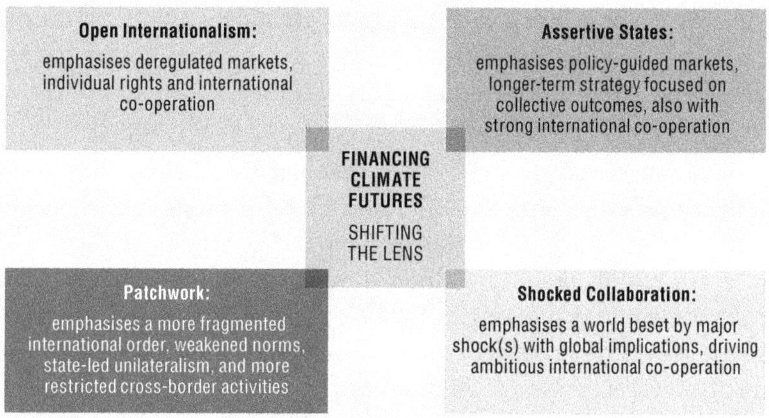

The key insights from this exercise focus on:

- **Long-term time horizon:** There is no substitute for explicit, long-term planning; governments and their agents, and less so market actors, are likely to be at the core of such long-termism.
- **Policy-guided finance:** Significant policy guidance and support to ensure that private financial markets can fulfil their key role in investing in climate-compatible infrastructure.
- **Citizen action:** Citizens can impact the financing of climate-compatible infrastructure but, going forward, are as likely to constrain as to enable progress, given their varied priorities and time horizons.
- **Resilient investment:** Strong government- and policy-directed finance will be required in the face of economic downturns and external shocks, which are inevitable over the period in question.
- **Shifting globalisation:** The combined effects of automation, climate, business model innovation and reinforcing policy may drive us towards higher fragmentation of the global economy, reshaping the demand for infrastructure, and increasing the importance of local financing solutions.
- **International co-operation:** International co-operation is key, but may become more effective when faced with significant shocks to the global economy.

Scenarios reinforce the importance of examining political will and the institutional and behavioural norms that inform investment decisions in climate-compatible infrastructure by governments, market actors and civil society. Overcoming distortions in decision making will likely make a significant difference to the pace and form of investment in climate-compatible infrastructure:

- Risk pricing needs to be more sensitised to complex and critical uncertainties, including through the use of scenario planning rather than exclusively singular, probability analysis.
- Capabilities need to be enhanced to better handle decision making under uncertainty all along the investment value chain, including investors through to procurement.
- Incentives need to be shifted, together with institutional norms, to increase the rate of adoption of a new generation of technologically intensive infrastructure and associated business and financing approaches.

Source: UN Environment (2018[25]), *Shifting the Lens.*

Moving away from our historic reliance on fossil fuels is necessary to anticipate any negative impacts from climate change, but implies also profound changes to the shape of our economies. Our societies, economies, policies and infrastructure have been hard-wired in the past decades to a growth model based on fossil fuels (OECD, 2015[22]). Inevitably, an economy-wide transformation is likely to generate tension among those who benefit from these changes and those who consider themselves worse off (OECD, 2017[3]).

An inclusive approach to the low-emission transition needs to be managed at two-levels (Fay et al., 2015[21]). First, it is essential that the transition benefits everyone, and does not impact the poor disproportionately. National and local policies that aim to reduce emissions and adapt to climate change have a range of economic and distributional consequences on households. In the absence of compensation policies, core climate policies have the potential to affect household spending and the affordability of energy, transport services, and housing, particularly for low-income households (OECD, 2018[29]) (see Chapter 7).

Second, it is also necessary to support and manage the transition for those individuals and communities that may be particularly affected as economies shift away from fossil fuels, such as those in heavy industrial regions and energy-intensive activities facing unemployment like coal workers. Ensuring that there are no stranded communities is as important to the transition as minimising the risk and cost of stranded assets. From historic examples like the coal mine closures of the 1980s in the United Kingdom, the delocalisation of heavy industry sectors such as steel production in the United States and shipbuilding in Japan, to the digitalisation of today, structural changes with competitiveness and employment impacts have raised concerns and resistance on the part of affected industries and workers (Botta, 2018[30]). There are also lessons to be learnt from recent transitions in sectors such as coal mining, where much of the transition has been driven by economic realities as much as by environmental considerations (Spencer, Sartor and Caldecott, 2017[31]).

For many industrial regions, managing a just transition requires developing strategies to support the reorientation of existing industries in order to increase their efficiency and lessen dependence on fossil fuels. For policy makers it also requires minimising the destruction of asset value and ensuring an orderly evolution. Targeted support is needed to compensate for economic loss. Structural reforms such as ensuring flexible labour markets and strengthening social protection schemes could also be instrumental in facilitating the transition, and overcoming political economy issues (see Chapter 4).

1.3. An agenda for transformation

This report lays out the agenda for a low-emission, resilient transformation that requires action across six areas: planning, innovation, budgeting, finance, development and cities. Different country contexts, resource endowments and capabilities will determine the priority areas for individual countries. In all countries, however, it is critical that a whole-of-government and whole-of-society approach is employed, with a central role to be played by ministries of finance and economy. This will help to ensure that the planning, investment and finance systems in place are "fit for the future" and able to smooth the path towards low-emission, resilient economies.

1. *Plan infrastructure for a low-emission and resilient future*

Long-term strategies can be formidable tools for governments and non-state actors to create consensus on their economic trajectories, provide long-term signals to markets and inform near-term policy and investment decisions. Infrastructure planning must be improved at all levels of government to create pipelines of sustainable infrastructure projects aligned with long-term climate and development objectives. Priority actions include:

- Develop new institutional configurations to align infrastructure plans with a long-term low-emission, resilient development vision.
- Make resilience the norm to limit vulnerability to climate damages, mainstream nature-based solutions and demand-management tools into planning to ensure a resilient future.
- Future-proof infrastructure investment decisions through approaches such as strategic foresight to monitor emerging socioeconomic and technological changes and regularly adjust long-term strategies.

2. *Unleash innovation to accelerate the transition*

To deliver the economic transformation required to address climate change, governments must accelerate the deployment of existing technologies, business models and services, and swiftly move the next generation of climate solutions from the lab to the market. To scale up climate solutions, governments should:

- Deploy targeted innovation policies to create and shape markets for climate innovations.
- Scale up public investment in research and development to create the next generation of climate solutions.
- Overcome the financial barriers to demonstration and early-stage commercialisation to bring existing technologies to scale.
- Promote international technology diffusion to ensure innovation benefits all.

3. *Ensure fiscal sustainability for a low-emission, resilient future*

The power and influence of public budgets, if channelled towards climate objectives, can provide significant momentum towards building a low-emission, resilient economic future. In order to make meaningful progress on climate, there are four priority policy actions:

- Diversify government revenue streams to prepare for carbon neutrality in the long run, and reduce governments' exposure to incumbents and vested interests in fossil fuel technologies.
- Align fiscal and budgetary incentives with climate objectives to discourage emissions-intensive behaviours or investments by economic actors.
- Leverage public procurement practices and indirect spending through state-owned enterprises, development finance institutions, export credit agencies and public investments to align with climate objectives.
- Ensure an inclusive transition along the way, fostering public support for raising climate ambition.

4. *Reset the financial system in line with long-term climate risks and opportunities*

There is an urgent need to mobilise all sources of private finance to scale up and shift infrastructure investment towards low-emission, resilient projects. An array of rules governing the financial system favours the status quo and stands in the way of the necessary reallocation of capital. Decision-making processes are distorted by inadequate climate risk pricing, capabilities and biased incentives in the investment value chain. The following actions will help move sustainable finance from momentum to transformation:

- Encourage the integration of climate impact into investment decisions and strategies to improve climate-risk management strategies.

- Incentivise the disclosure of climate-related risks and opportunities for investors to increase transparency in financial markets.
- Support financial supervisory authority to better assess and manage climate-related risks that could threaten the financial stability of the system in the short and long term.

5. *Rethink development finance for climate*

While many different actors will need to be mobilised to help address the sustainable infrastructure challenge, development banks and development finance institutions are critical, particularly in developing country contexts. But for these banks to play a transformational role, they need to do more to integrate climate into underlying development objectives, better align overall portfolios with the Paris Agreement and scale up efforts to unlock commercial investment. Development banks cannot do this alone – their activities are dependent on, and strongly influenced by shareholder and client governments. Scaling up climate action requires governments and development banks to make three key changes:

- Strengthen development banks' mandates and incentives to deliver transformative climate action.
- Bring new investors and sources of finance to investments to create new climate markets.
- Use concessional finance to enable development banks to drive the transformation.

6. *Empower city governments to build low-emission and resilient urban societies*

Empowering local and city governments to plan and finance low-emission, resilient infrastructure is an essential part of achieving climate and development goals. The way cities expand and develop will determine the emissions of 70% of the world's population in the 2050. Cities are particularly vulnerable to climate risks and must develop strategies that ensure urban resilience. The failure to invest in the right urban forms will put residents, the local economy and social cohesion at risk, potentially exacerbating existing inequalities. National and local governments should work together to pursue the following transformative actions:

- Rethink institutional configurations to integrate land-use and transport strategies and seize the immediate development benefits of low-emission, resilient planning.
- Align national and local fiscal policies to encourage and enable low-emission, resilient investments and behaviours.
- Build climate-related and project finance capacity in cities to efficiently finance and deliver complex low-emission, resilient infrastructure projects.
- Seize the social and economic benefits of low-emission, resilient planning to deliver inclusive urban growth.

Notes

1. As measured using the international poverty line, i.e. USD 1.90 a day at 2011 purchasing power parity.
2. The combined dataset covers 76 national economies that collectively contribute 94% of global CO_2 emissions.

References

Botta, E. (2018), "A Review of "Transition Management" Strategies: Lessons for Advancing the Green Low-carbon Transition", *Green Growth and Sustainable Development Forum 2018 Issue Notes*, OECD Publishing, Paris, *http://www.oecd.org/greengrowth/ggsd-2018/*. [30]

European Commission (2018), *Press release - Frequently asked questions: Commission proposals on financing sustainable growth*, *http://europa.eu/rapid/press-release_MEMO-18-3730_en.htm* (accessed on 12 September 2018). [11]

Fay, M. et al. (2015), *Decarbonizing Development: Three Steps to a Zero-Carbon Future*, World Bank, *https://openknowledge.worldbank.org/handle/10986/21842*. [21]

G20 Green Finance Study Group (2016), *G20 Green Finance Synthesis Report*, G20 Green Finance Study Group, *http://www.g20.utoronto.ca/2016/green-finance-synthesis.pdf* (accessed on 12 September 2018). [18]

Hallegatte, S. et al. (2016), *Shock Waves: Climate Change and Development Series Managing the Impacts of Climate Change on Poverty*, World Bank, Washington, DC, *https://openknowledge.worldbank.org/bitstream/handle/10986/22787/9781464806735.pdf* (accessed on 27 September 2018). [5]

IEA (2018), *Global Energy and CO2 Status Report 2017*, International Energy Agency, Paris, *http://www.iea.org/publications/freepublications/publication/GECO2017.pdf*. [14]

IEA (2018), *World Energy Investment 2018*, International Energy Agency, Paris, *https://www.iea.org/wei2018/*. [10]

IEA (2017), *Digitalization and Energy*, International Energy Agency, Paris, *http://www.iea.org/publications/freepublications/publication/DigitalizationandEnergy3.pdf* (accessed on 05 July 2018). [8]

IPCC (2018), *Global Warming of 1.5 degrees C*, Intergovernmental Panel on Climate Change, Geneva, *http://www.ipcc.ch/report/sr15/*. [1]

Maimbo, S. et al. (2017), "Roadmap for a Sustainable Financial System", No. 121283, World Bank Group and UNEP Inquiry, Washington, DC, *http://documents.worldbank.org/curated/en/903601510548466486/Roadmap-for-a-sustainable-financial-system*. [24]

New Climate Economy (2016), *The Sustainable Infrastructure Imperative: Financing for Better Growth and Development*, The New Climate Economy, Washington, DC and London, *http://newclimateeconomy.report/2016/wp-content/uploads/sites/4/2014/08/NCE_2016Report.pdf* (accessed on 17 October 2018). [2]

OECD (2018), *Effective Carbon Rates 2018*, OECD Publishing, Paris, *https://one.oecd.org/document/COM/ENV/EPOC/CTPA/CFA(2018)1/REV1/en/pdf* (accessed on 19 July 2018). [16]

OECD (2018), *Inclusive Growth in Seoul, Korea*, OECD Publishing, Paris, *http://dx.doi.org/10.1787/9789264290198-en*. [29]

OECD (2018), *OECD Companion to the Inventory of Support Measures for Fossil Fuels 2018*, OECD Publishing, Paris, *http://dx.doi.org/10.1787/9789264286061-en*. [17]

OECD (2017), *Investing in Climate, Investing in Growth*, OECD Publishing, Paris, *http://dx.doi.org/10.1787/9789264273528-en*. [3]

OECD (2015), *Aligning Policies for a Low-carbon Economy*, OECD Publishing, Paris, *http://dx.doi.org/10.1787/9789264233294-en*. [22]

Rigaud, K. et al. (2018), *Groundswell: Preparing for Internal Climate Migration*, World Bank, Washington, DC, *http://hdl.handle.net/10986/29461* (accessed on 19 October 2018). [6]

Röttgers, D. and B. Anderson (2018), "Drivers and barriers to the decarbonisation of the electricity sector (forthcoming)", *OECD Environment Working Papers*, OECD Publishing, Paris, *http://dx.doi.org/10.1787/19970900*. [26]

Spencer, T., O. Sartor and B. Caldecott (2017), *Lessons from previous 'coal transitions'*, IDDRI, Paris, *https://www.iddri.org/en/publications-and-events/report/lessons-previous-coal-transitions* (accessed on 26 October 2018). [31]

TCFD (2017), *Recommendations of the Task Force on Climate-related Financial Disclosures*, *https://www.fsb-tcfd.org/wp-content/uploads/2017/06/FINAL-TCFD-Report-062817.pdf* (accessed on 12 September 2018). [13]

Thomä, J., S. Dupré and M. Fulton (2018), "The Bigger Picture: The Impact of Automation, AI, Shared Economy... On Oil Demand", No. 2018/2, 2 Degrees Investing Initiative, *https://2degrees-investing.org/wp-content/uploads/2018/05/2dii_Disruption_v1.pdf* (accessed on 17 July 2018). [7]

UN Economic and Social Council (2018), *Progress towards the Sustainable Development Goals*, UN Economic and Social Council, New York City, *http://undocs.org/E/2018/64* (accessed on 19 October 2018). [4]

UN Environment (2018), *Shifting the Lens (forthcoming)*, UN Environment, *https://www.unepinquiry.org*. [25]

UNDESA (2015), "Risks of Exposure and Vulnerability to Natural Disasters at the City Level: A Global Overview", *https://esa.un.org/Unpd/Wup/Publications/Files/WUP2014-Technical Paper-NaturalDisaster.pdf* (accessed on 25 July 2018). [27]

UNEP (2017), *The Emissions Gap Report 2017*, UN Environment Programme (UNEP), Nairobi, *https://wedocs.unep.org/bitstream/handle/20.500.11822/22070/EGR_2017.pdf*. [15]

UNEP Inquiry (2018), *Making Waves: Aligning the Financial System with Sustainable Development*, UN Environment, Geneva, *http://unepinquiry.org/making-waves/*. [12]

UNEP Inquiry (2015), *The Financial System We Need: Aligning the Financial System with Sustainable Development*, UN Environment, *http://www.unep.org/inquiry* (accessed on 12 September 2018). [23]

UNFCCC (2015), *The Paris Agreement*, *https://unfccc.int/process-and-meetings/the-paris-agreement/the-paris-agreement* (accessed on 08 June 2018). [20]

World Bank and Ecofys (2018), *State and Trends of Carbon Pricing 2018*, World Bank, Washington, DC, *https://openknowledge.worldbank.org/handle/10986/29687*. [9]

Financing Climate Futures
Rethinking Infrastructure

Chapter 2

Plan infrastructure for a low-emission and resilient future

The transition towards low-emission, resilient economies presupposes far-reaching changes to infrastructure, technology and industrial systems that will require prudent planning. This chapter makes the case for improved planning practices as a prerequisite for successfully delivering on both climate and development objectives. It identifies barriers for implementing changes and emerging good practices in reconciling long-term climate and development objectives with near-term demand for infrastructure services. The chapter outlines three priority actions: develop new institutional configurations to align today's decisions with long-term objectives, ensure that resilience to the impacts of climate change is a central component of planning, and harness the benefits of foresight to complement climate models in strategic planning.

Key messages

Long-term strategies can be formidable tools for governments and non-state actors to create consensus on their economic trajectories, provide long-term signals to markets and inform near-term policy and investment decisions. Infrastructure planning must be improved at all levels of government to create pipelines of sustainable infrastructure projects aligned with long-term climate and development objectives. Priority actions include:

- Develop new institutional configurations to align infrastructure plans with a long-term low-emission, resilient development vision.
- Make resilience the norm to limit vulnerability to climate damages, mainstream nature-based solutions and demand-management tools into planning to ensure a resilient future.
- Future-proof infrastructure investment decisions through approaches such as strategic foresight to monitor emerging socioeconomic and technological changes and regularly adjust long-term strategies.

Why is improved planning transformative?

Success in limiting global temperature rise to well-below 2°C and towards 1.5°C hinges on rapid and unprecedented transformations of infrastructure stocks in energy, land-use and industrial systems worldwide (IPCC, 2018[1]). While the emission reductions pledged in countries' 2030 Nationally Determined Contributions (NDCs) can be achieved with current infrastructure systems, post-2030 decarbonisation pathways that meet the Paris Agreement temperature goals will require far-reaching changes to infrastructure, technology and industrial systems. Such radical shifts require better planning practices that align short-term infrastructure investment plans and strategies with long-term climate and development goals.

The Paris Agreement recognises the importance of long-term planning in Article 4.19, which calls on countries to "formulate and communicate long-term low greenhouse gas emission development strategies, mindful of Article 2". Such long-term strategies can help countries scale up the ambition of their NDCs, which has been inadequate to date, and reconcile decisions in the present with long-term climate goals.

Given the long lifespan of infrastructure assets, the alignment of today's infrastructure choices with long-term targets is essential, since what countries build today will determine their emissions and vulnerability to a changing climate for decades to come. If they plan prudently, countries can wean their economies off dependence on fossil fuels and ensure that financing flows towards low-emission, resilient infrastructure projects. Such planning can identify and exploit synergies between climate and economic development goals to foster public support for the transition.

Otherwise, countries risk building infrastructure assets that would inevitably face stranding – i.e. retirement before the end of their economic lifecycle – and lock their economies into elevated future emissions and costly path dependencies. Not only are investments in emissions-intensive infrastructure risky and possibly unprofitable, they also attract capital that could otherwise support and scale up infrastructure compatible with climate objectives.

What is the state of play?

Governments face the dual challenge of planning infrastructure that satisfies the immediate demand of their citizens for services like energy and mobility while simultaneously meeting long-term climate goals. On both counts, business-as-usual planning practices have underperformed, leading to severe underinvestment in infrastructure systems globally and sluggish action to mainstream resilience and curb emissions.

Some countries are beginning to develop long-term low-emission development strategies and systematically integrate climate considerations in infrastructure planning, but they remain the exception rather than the rule. To date, only ten of the UNFCCC's 197 parties have submitted long-term low-emission development strategies: Benin, Canada, the Czech Republic, France, Germany, the Marshall Islands, Mexico, Ukraine, the United Kingdom and the United States (UNFCCC[2]). A 2015 survey led by the G20 Investment and Infrastructure Working Group revealed an uneven mainstreaming of climate change in infrastructure planning across sectors: nine G20 countries include both climate mitigation and adaptation considerations, while a further four only take account of mitigation concerns. Five countries did not take into account neither climate mitigation nor adaptation (OECD, 2017[3]).

The incompatibility of current infrastructure planning with the Paris Agreement's goals and other development goals is evident in many ways:

- **Energy:** The majority of global electricity continues to derive from fossil fuels, and investment flows still overwhelmingly favour fossil fuel supply over renewable electricity generation (IEA, 2018[4]). Looking at coal power plants alone, total lifecycle emissions from all plants currently operating or under development would be high enough to put both the 2°C and 1.5°C temperature goals out of reach. This means many projects will need to be cancelled and existing plants will face early retirement (Shearer et al., 2018[5]).
- **Agriculture, forestry and other land-use (AFOLU):** Countries must strike a balance between food production, biodiversity conservation and other needs while managing the sector's sizeable impact on emissions. Innovation and investment have been insufficient in more efficient production techniques and supply chains, which could relieve pressure to convert forests and other land for crops and reduce food waste and loss. As various elements — such as population growth, greater per capita caloric intake, greater demand for resource — and land-intensive meat and dairy products strain existing systems, current practices could lead to suboptimal crop yield improvements and sustained food price increases in the long term (FAO, 2018[6]).
- **Cities:** Urban sprawl has increased since 1990 in most OECD countries. This promotes dependency on cars for mobility, which worsens air pollution, and contributes to environmental challenges through increased emissions as well as biodiversity and ecosystem loss (see Chapter 7) (OECD, 2018[7]).

What are the opportunities and barriers for change?

Long-term strategies can be formidable tools for governments and non-state actors to create consensus on the direction of travel of their economies, provide long-term signals to markets and to inform near-term policy and investment decisions. However, political pressure to deliver services for development goals in the short and medium terms can predispose governments to pursue development pathways based on well-established infrastructure assets. This, therefore, impedes the required shifts in infrastructure stocks towards low-emission, resilient alternatives and delays climate action.

In addition to the lack of long-term infrastructure planning aligned with climate objectives, a prominent barrier to accelerating investment in low-emission, resilient infrastructure is the lack of investor-ready, bankable infrastructure projects that are compatible with a low-emission, resilient future (Nassiry, Nakhooda and Barnard, 2016[8]). Many governments are constrained by a lack of capacities to integrate climate concerns in infrastructure planning and assessment. Institutional structures and incentives currently prevent the adoption of a cross-sectoral, whole-of-government perspective in long-term development strategies as well as infrastructure and climate action plans. Behavioural and data biases encourage choices that are in line with historical practices rather than potential emerging alternatives (Röttgers and Anderson, 2018[9]).

To deliver the transformation needed and help unlock financial flows towards low-emission, resilient infrastructure, countries should develop clear infrastructure investment plans that take mitigation and adaptation objectives into account, as part of their work on long-term low-emission development pathways. Ensuring that infrastructure investments are flexible and robust against a different set of socioeconomic uncertainties is an essential part of building resilience into the system.

2.1. Plan infrastructure in the present with long-term climate goals in mind

Decisions made today, particularly for infrastructure assets with long lifecycles, can either contribute to or hinder efforts to achieve the transition. Long-term planning needs to inform new courses of action in the present and planning in the near and medium terms. This requires aligning different time horizons: short-term plans need to be elaborated with a view to how they will affect long-term climate objectives, while also satisfying current needs.

Create long-term strategies with development and climate at their core

Long-term planning exercises, such as the long-term low-emission development strategies recommended by Article 4.19 of the Paris Agreement, need to become the norm across all countries to prepare adequately for the global transition towards a low-emission, resilient future. Development finance institutions (DFIs) have begun mainstreaming long-term climate concerns into their operations (see Box 2.1), and several multi-stakeholder initiatives have emerged to help countries elaborate and implement their long-term strategies. These include the "2050 Facility", created by the *Agence française de développement* (AFD); the Deep Decarbonisation Pathways Project (DDPP), led by the Institute for Sustainable Development and International Relations (IDDRI) and the Sustainable Development Solutions Network (SDSN); and the 2050 Pathways Platform, launched at COP 22 in Marrakesh. The 2050 Pathways Platform aims to support countries' efforts to develop long-term development pathways in line with the goals of the Paris Agreement, and it has published key principles for developing these strategies (see Box 2.2). These principles stress the importance of reconciling climate action with socioeconomic development objectives and crafting the strategies with input from all stakeholders across sectors, industries and ministerial portfolios (2050 Pathways Platform, 2017[10]). Crucially, the platform not only encourages national governments to undertake this exercise but also cities, subnational governments and companies.[1]

Box 2.1. **2050 Pathways: Integrating long-term climate goals into World Bank operations**

The World Bank is committed to transforming its own operations and aligning its support to countries to help them meet their climate goals. In 2016, the World Bank presented its Climate Change Action Plan and is well on track to meet its targets. In line with countries submitting updated and potentially more ambitious NDCs, the World Bank will present a stock-take of its Climate Change Action Plan and announce new commitments and targets beyond 2020 at COP24 in Poland in 2018.

As an institution, the World Bank recognised that it needs to go even further and undertake more transformative changes to meet the long-term objectives of the Paris Agreement. Therefore, the World Bank engaged in a visioning exercise to explore what long-term low-emission and climate-resilient development pathways might look like (using a 2050 timeframe) in key sectors and countries where the institution is active. The exercise is helping to identify what could be potential implications for the way the World Bank does business, such as introducing new types of services and financial instruments, and integrating long-term dimensions in country engagement strategies and project.

A strategic vision of infrastructure's role in national development that runs across ministerial portfolios allows both the connections between infrastructure for energy, transport, water and other sectors, as well as the co-benefits (such as improved health outcomes) to be exploited. This helps to create synergies, reduce inefficiencies and foster support for the transition. There are more synergies between mitigation efforts that are in line with 1.5°C pathways and the Sustainable Development Goals (SDGs) than there are possible trade-offs. The co-benefits are particularly sizeable for SDGs 3 (health), 7 (clean energy), 11 (cities and communities), 12 (responsible consumption and production) and 14 (oceans). Prudent planning can also help avoid possible trade-offs arising from competition between, for instance, food production and measures supporting afforestation and bioenergy supply (IPCC, 2018[1]).

Existing national pathways offer similar insights into synergies between climate action and broader sustainable development questions. China's Deep Decarbonisation Pathway created by the DDPP, for instance, demonstrates how prudent planning for decarbonisation across industry, transport and energy could dramatically reduce China's emissions while reducing primary air pollutants in major Chinese cities to meet World Health Organisation air quality standards (Liu et al., 2015[11]; Waisman et al., 2015[12]). South Africa's Deep Decarbonisation Pathway, meanwhile, uses scenarios to address political economy concerns resulting from the necessary shift of labour away from the country's coal mining industry towards other sectors. In one scenario, the structure of the economy transforms so that low-emission sectors such as furniture, glass and forestry absorb low-skill workers; in another, an improved educational system provides the necessary educated labour to shift the economy towards high-skill low-emission sectors (Altieri et al., 2015[13]).

Such whole-of-government planning, however, is not yet standard practice. According to an OECD survey, only about half of OECD countries reported having a strategy for infrastructure that covers all sectors (OECD, 2018[14]). In addition to cross-sector synergies, mainstreaming climate change considerations in infrastructure plans is essential to achieve long-term goals. However, the extent to which climate change is considered within countries' infrastructure objectives and long-term plans varies considerably (ITF, 2017[15]).

Box 2.2. **Principles and building blocks of the 2050 Pathways Platform**

Principles: A general approach to 2050 pathways analysis, based on the principles below, is recommended for producing pathways that meet the criteria of clarity, relevance, practicality and credibility.

- Socioeconomic and emissions objectives are incorporated side by side as integral parts of the analysis.
- Backcasting is used starting with the desired long-term goal and working backwards to the present to shed light on key decision points and trade-offs.
- Analysis focuses on the physical transformations required to meet long-term emissions and socioeconomic goals.
- Pathways development engages stakeholders in the analysis and promotes communication of the findings.
- Policy questions, objectives and boundary conditions of the analysis are defined at the outset and the analytical toolkit is selected accordingly.

Building blocks: The principles of 2050 pathways are embodied in three building blocks of the pathways design process.

- Creation of narratives describing possible futures.
- Analysis and modelling of scenarios based on those narratives.
- Use of dashboards for communicating modelling assumptions and results.

Source: 2050 Pathways Platform (2017[10]), *2050 Pathways: A Handbook.*

Build capacity and techniques to link near-term action with long-term climate targets

A key component of success in achieving the Paris Agreement's objectives relates to building climate-related capacities in governments. This includes climate modelling capacities, to understand whether current infrastructure decisions are compatible with carbon budgets and the emissions reduction trajectories of long-term plans. For instance, the United Kingdom has set a 2050 target of reducing emissions by 80% compared to 1990 levels. It has charged the Committee on Climate Change with translating this target into a carbon budget over five-year segments, which are then assigned to individual sectors (OECD, 2018[16]). This creates the necessary link between national long-term targets and the decision-making process in the shorter term.

Models that project current trends into the future are helpful, but decision makers can also employ 'backcasting' to determine which proposed policies or infrastructure projects are compatible with long-term science-based targets. In backcasting, rather than starting from present trends, modellers begin with the desired outcome (e.g. national emissions reduction goals) and work backwards to construct a plausible pathway to achieve it. The approach can be used to identify misalignments between present actions and long-term objectives in policy, infrastructure and investment. It can also shed light on practices that contribute to incremental emissions abatement but that are incompatible with long-term targets (2050 Pathways Platform, 2017[17]).

It is critical that countries' emission reduction pledges in the mid-term are consistent with net-zero emission longer-term goals. While NDCs adopt a 5- or 10-year view with the most recent iterations covering up to 2030, infrastructure assets are often in operation for several decades so their potential impact on emissions and climate go far beyond what NDCs can capture. New coal-fired power plants could, for example, be compatible with energy access objectives and even with 2030 NDCs in certain countries, but over the course of such plants' lifetimes the total emissions would be incompatible with the global goal of achieving net-zero emissions by the second half of the century (ClimateWorks Australia, 2017[18]). Infrastructure investments on a very large scale, like China's Belt and Road Initiative, offer a unique opportunity to ensure that projects align with low-emission pathways (see Box 2.3).

Box 2.3. **Infrastructure built as part of the Belt and Road Initiative will shape recipient countries' future emissions**

China's Belt and Road Initiative (BRI), a large-scale infrastructure development strategy, will involve the world's single largest flow of infrastructure financing and build out ever. It covers more than 68 countries, including 65% of the world's population and 40% of the global GDP. Its investments in infrastructure already amount to USD 690 billion and further commitments will total USD 1.5 trillion by 2025. However, the BRI will only account for a small fraction of total infrastructure investment in recipient countries.

Which infrastructure projects receive financing from the initiative will shape future emissions. Current infrastructure investment patterns in recipient countries are emissions-intensive. Over 50% of planned BRI investments in the power sector are coal-based. Without a major shift in the infrastructure profile, especially in power and transport, aggregate emissions across recipient countries could be several times those of China itself by 2040, effectively putting the Paris Agreement's temperature goals out of reach.

BRI recipient countries could adopt more ambitious growth pathways towards emissions reduction and climate resilience, with major gains possible by embracing existing best-in-class power and transport technologies and infrastructure. The BRI could support this positive deviation from the current trajectory, both through aligning investments with more ambitious climate goals, and related support, such as the greening of domestic financial systems through which an even larger share of the overall investments will flow.

Source: UN Environment (2018[19]), Greening the Belt and Road Initiative (forthcoming).

Create pipelines of bankable infrastructure projects in line with climate objectives

It is essential that investments stop flowing towards projects incompatible with the Paris Agreement's goals. As an alternative to emissions-intensive assets, countries should identify and promote projects that meet development needs and align with their long-term objectives and NDCs. Together, these infrastructure projects should form a 'pipeline' of projects for investment to streamline the process between project conception and financing. To create such pipelines, governments and public institutions must develop detailed infrastructure investment plans and integrate them into the national priority context. This can help create clear signals to investors as to where investments should flow (OECD, 2018[16]).

One emerging good practice is Colombia's Strategic Projects of National Interest (PINES, *Proyectos estratégicos de interés nacional*). These consist of projects proposed by both the public and private sectors, which are assessed by relevant ministries against their sectoral priorities. The most appropriate proposals undergo further scrutiny by the Inter-Sectoral Commission on Infrastructure and Strategic Projects, chaired by the Minister of Transport and composed of Ministers with diverse portfolios: Interior Affairs, Finance and Public Credit, Mines and Energy, and Environment and Sustainable Development. Technical committees assist by evaluating environmental and other aspects of proposals (OECD, 2018[16]).

Another practical way to support pipeline development is to create entities dedicated to this purpose. For example, the EU High-Level Expert Group on Sustainable Finance (HLEG) has proposed to establish Sustainable Infrastructure Europe, which would provide advice, improve capacity and reduce regulatory uncertainty for EU member states (2018[20]). These dedicated entities would convene and link up key actions and host information that could help countries estimate their infrastructure needs and translate them into clear project pipelines.

Existing public financial institutions and entities could also be used to support better pipeline development. In developing countries that may lack in-house capacities, initiatives such as the NDC Partnership[2] can enhance co-operation and provide technical and financial support to enable countries to set climate targets as soon as possible. Initiatives led by development finance institutions, such as the *Agence française de développement* (AFD) and the Inter-American Development Bank (IDB), now help countries screen projects for climate risks. Governments can also use their export credit facilities and official development assistance providers to encourage better infrastructure pipelines that are aligned with the objectives of the Paris Agreement (OECD, 2017[3]). Domestically, green investment banks, which are public financial institutions dedicated to green investment, could be developed or expanded to support the development of pipelines as part of their mandate (OECD, 2016[21]).

2.2. Make resilient infrastructure the norm, not the exception

There is an urgent need to strengthen existing and build new infrastructure that can respond more adequately to the risks and impacts of a changing climate. Climate change poses a number of threats to economic development, with rising sea levels, increased risk of drought in some areas, shifting rainfall patterns and greater prevalence of temperature extremes, including a change in the intensity and frequency of extreme events. In 2017, Hurricane Irma illustrated the major damage that can be caused by extreme weather events, leaving 6.7 million customers without electricity (EIA, 2017[22]). Choosing inclusive, climate-resilient approaches to infrastructure provision at the outset will help to moderate the extent of those negative impacts. The World Bank estimates that "building back better" after disasters could save up to USD 173 billion per year globally in well-being losses due to natural disasters, compared to business as usual (see Box 2.4).

Countries are making progress towards integrating resilience in infrastructure investment. This is evident through an increased number of measures to strengthen the enabling environment for infrastructure resilience: providing climate information, integrating climate risks into technical standards, and encouraging physical climate risk disclosure (see Chapter 5) (Vallejo and Mullan, 2017[24]). In addition, the volume of development finance targeting adaptation, although small, has been increasing. For example, adaptation financing from the multilateral development banks (MDBs) increased from USD 5.9 billion in 2016 to USD 6.8 billion in 2017.[3]

Despite these promising developments, several barriers continue to prevent the alignment of financial flows with resilience. The impacts from climate change often lie beyond the time horizons considered by investors and other decision makers. Further complications include a lack of information, capacity and tools; policy misalignments and market failures; and insufficient weighting given to climate risks. There remains an urgent need to scale up action in a manner commensurate with the threat posed by climate change.

Box 2.4. **Building more resilient infrastructure in the wake of natural disasters is a good investment**

Disaster losses tend to disproportionately affect poor people. The Caribbean hurricane season of 2017 was a tragic illustration of this. Two category 5 hurricanes wreaked destruction on numerous small islands, causing severe damage on islands like Barbuda, Dominica and Saint Martin. The human cost of these disasters was immense, and the impact of this devastation was felt most strongly by poorer communities in the path of the storms.

Yet, amidst the destruction, it is essential to look forward and to build back better. Countries can strengthen their resilience to natural shocks through a better reconstruction process. Reconstruction needs to be strong, so that assets and livelihoods become less vulnerable to future shocks; fast, so that people can get back to their normal life as early as possible; and inclusive, so that nobody is left behind in the recovery process.

The World Bank report *Building Back Better: Achieving Resilience through Stronger, Faster, and More Inclusive Post-Disaster Reconstruction* estimates that the benefits of building back better could be very large: up to USD 173 billion per year globally. They would be greatest among the communities and countries that are hit by disasters most intensely and frequently and that have limited coverage of social protection and financial inclusion. Small island states – because of their size, exposure, and vulnerability – are among the countries where building back better has the greatest potential. A stronger, faster and more inclusive recovery would lead to an average reduction in disaster-related well-being losses of 59% in the 17 small island states covered in the report.

Source: Hallegatte, S., J. Rentschler, B. Walsh (2018[23]), *Building Back Better: Achieving Resilience through Stronger, Faster, and More Inclusive Post-Disaster Reconstruction.*

Reshape demand for infrastructure services

A key action for greater resilience would be to fill the investment gap and mobilise additional resources for projects that enhance adaptive capacity, strengthen resilience and reduce vulnerability. This can be achieved, in part, through new technologies and better data, as well as by influencing the behaviour and investments of infrastructure users and beneficiaries.

These demand-side measures can help to reduce the likelihood of the failure of service provision or reduce the negative consequences when disruption occurs. An increasing number of examples are showing how they can be implemented:

- *Energy:* New technologies, including smart meters and improvements in battery storage, hold the potential to increase domestic users' contribution to grid reliability. In the Netherlands, the Eneco Crowdnett is aggregating home batteries to provide a "virtual power station". There have been early studies of aggregating the batteries of electric vehicles in a similar manner.
- *Transport:* In Seoul, Korea an intelligent traffic management system (TOPIS) provides real-time monitoring of traffic conditions throughout the city. Information gathered is provided to end users through signs, website and mobile apps. The system is open to third parties, thereby stimulating the development of private markets for resilience.
- *Water:* In England, water companies are pursuing a "carrot-and-stick" approach to reduce water consumption, reducing the risk of drought. South East Water covers a severe water-stressed area, and is implementing compulsory metering combined with the provision of free water-saving technologies (such as low-flow showerheads).

Increase the use of nature-based solutions

Nature-based solutions are increasingly being used as a complement or replacement for traditional grey infrastructure, particularly in the area of water and coastal management (Jones, Hole and Zavaleta, 2012[25]). These measures have the potential to be significantly cheaper: the City of Copenhagen found that the use of nature-based solutions, such as more green spaces, to cope with heavy downpours would be DKK 7 billion (EUR 940 million) cheaper than reliance upon grey infrastructure alone. Analysis in Portland, Maine found that nature-based approaches to water treatment, such as afforestation and reforestation, would be 51–76% cheaper than a treatment plant (Talberth et al., 2012[26]). As well as being cheaper, these approaches could also yield co-benefits such as amenity value, carbon sequestration and provision of species' habitats.

Nature-based solutions are being used by a range of actors at various scales to improve their resilience to the climate:

- **Shanghai, China "Sponge City"** – Shanghai has been selected as one of 30 "sponge cities", which are to use nature-based solutions to reduce flood risk. A combination of measures including permeable paving, green roofs and rain gardens are being installed to ensure that 70% of storm water runoff is captured, reused or absorbed. The national government is covering 20% of the cost, with the remainder expected to be provided from local governments and private investors.
- **Dow Chemicals "Valuing Nature" initiative** – This company now screens all new capital, R&D and property decisions to identify opportunities for using nature. In 2017, they estimated that the implementation of nature-based solutions under this initiative had led to savings or new cash flow of USD 120 million. Initiatives included the installation of green retaining walls at their site in Aratu, Brazil instead of concrete walls. This approach helps to combat erosion while also reducing surface run-off. This programme is being funded from the company's own resources (Dow, 2017[27]).
- **Quintana Roo, Mexico "Coastal Zone Management Trust"** – Healthy coastal reefs play an essential role in protecting coastal assets against storms. It has been estimated that they can absorb 97% of wave energy from storm surges. This fund combines taxes collected from the local tourist industry and local government funding to maintain the reefs. The fund also purchases insurance against damage to the reef, which then covers restoration activities following particularly severe storms (The Nature Conservancy, 2018[28]).

Nature-based solutions, predominantly in the land-use sector, also have important, cost-effective mitigation applications, through avoided deforestation and restoration of degraded lands, for instance. Policies in agriculture, forestry and other land use (AFOLU) can be used to maximise net emissions abatement by reducing emissions from land-use change and increasing the removal and sequestration of emissions (see Box 2.5).

Nature-based solutions are not a panacea, however, and will be better suited to managing some types of risks than others. Experience has shown that to realise their potential the design of these approaches needs to be tailored to the context of the climate risk. Poorly planned efforts may be worse than useless, failing to deliver the promised benefits of resilience and disrupting ecological systems. A range of guidance is now available for ensuring the effectiveness of these solutions as part of integrated strategies. This includes the World Bank's 2017 publication *Implementing nature-based flood protection: Principles and implementation guidance* (2017[29]).

Box 2.5. The land-use sector has great potential to remove and store atmospheric CO_2

How land is used is essential not only for climate resilience, but also for mitigation. In particular, avoiding deforestation and forest degradation, and restoring organic soils and degraded lands could contribute considerably to lower-emission pathways. In fact, all pathways consistent with limiting global temperature rise to below 1.5°C assume CO_2 removal of about 100-1 000 $GtCO_2$ this century.

While there remains a degree of uncertainty around the mitigation potential of the land-use sector, studies indicate that it is significant. The fifth assessment report of the Intergovernmental Panel on Climate Change (IPCC), for example, estimated the global abatement potential of restoring cultivated organic soils to be 248 $MtCO_2e$/year (at a cost of up to 20 USD/tCO_2e). A more recent analysis estimates that conservation, restoration and improved management of forests, grasslands and wetlands could deliver 23.8 $GtCO_2$ of emission reductions by 2030, even when accounting for food and fibre security and biodiversity conservation. About half of this mitigation potential represents cost-effective climate mitigation, defined as a marginal abatement cost of less than or equal to 100 USD per tonne of CO_2 by 2030. It is estimated that deploying these "natural climate solutions" could deliver up to 37% of the emission reductions needed by 2030 in order to have a greater than 66% likelihood of holding warming below 2°C and 20% of the emissions needed between now and 2050.

Source: IPCC (2018[1]), *Global Warming of 1.5°C*, Intergovernmental Panel on Climate Change, Geneva; Smith, P. et al. (Agriculture, Forestry and Other Land Use (AFOLU), 2014), "Agriculture, Forestry and Other Land Use (AFOLU)", *Climate Change 2014: Mitigation of Climate Change*; Griscom, B. et al. (2017[31]), "Natural Climate Solutions", *Proceedings of the National Academy of Sciences of the United States of America*, 114/44.

2.3. Use strategic foresight to improve decision making under uncertainty

It is impossible to predict precisely what the future will look like in 2050 or beyond, even with the most robust, finely calibrated models. Unexpected shocks – such as geopolitical upheaval or sudden technological breakthroughs – could have unforeseen impacts and disrupt those models' underlying assumptions. Models in the 1970s did not – and, indeed, could not have been expected to – predict the technological changes over the past 50 years; the current models can hardly be expected to capture the changes to come.

Strategic foresight is a useful tool for approaching decision making with such levels of uncertainty and complexity that can complement models by preparing for several plausible scenarios that could emerge from non-linear shocks. It considers points of uncertainty in the present and develops several plausible future scenarios stemming from them. Its insights can inform planning exercises across government agencies for both climate change mitigation and adaptation as a complement to models (see Box 2.6), and the approach has been used in the Financing Climate Futures initiative, notably in the *Shifting the Lens* report (see Box 1.1).

Develop strategic foresight capacity across government agencies

Dedicated strategic foresight teams can analyse possible emerging trends (called "weak signals") to predict how, at a larger scale, they could affect the future. The ability to do so is a key complement to traditional modelling exercises, as it captures the impacts of unexpected disruptions. Building additional capacity dedicated to strategic foresight and the integration of its insights into long-term planning exercises could ensure that the pathways against which current actions are compared adapt to emerging best available knowledge and possible future disruptions.

Box 2.6. Challenges in energy systems modelling

Energy systems models, often contained within broader integrated assessment models, are the dominant tool for exploring how energy systems could evolve under a variety of greenhouse gas (GHG) emissions constraints (IPCC, 2001[32]; IPCC, 2007[33]; IPCC, 2014[34]). They are invaluable in providing quantified answers on how to meet current and future energy demand without exceeding prescribed emissions constraints. In particular, they can provide key information, such as future demand for various fuel types, fuel trade between regions, carbon prices and sectoral energy prices consistent with their emissions pathways, and the degree of emissions permit trading between different regions with different emission constraints. These tools are also ideal for undertaking "experiments" with possible low-emission pathways, such as examining the economic costs of delayed mitigation action to achieve given climate targets (Rogelj et al., 2013[35]; Gambhir et al., 2017[36]; Riahi et al., 2015[37]).

While these models are the cornerstone of long-term low-emission development strategies, they would benefit from the insights of other complementary approaches. For example, the current generation of models cannot represent the invention of as-yet unknown technologies, or the emergence of fundamentally new behavioural or social patterns that may affect energy use. For example, the emergence of ultra-high-speed "hyperloops" (Palacin, 2016[38]) could conceivably replace a significant share of domestic aviation. The emergence of circular and shared economy business models could radically shift the demand for infrastructure moving forward.

The models also do not yet represent the costs and implications of investment in, and lock-in to, specific infrastructures, such as electric charging versus hydrogen transport infrastructure, which may reasonably be considered as alternative strategies for achieving low-emission road transport. Further, the sheer range of model outputs (such as carbon prices, rates of decarbonisation and technology mixes) in comparative studies of models – even where certain basic assumptions such as socioeconomic pathways are shared (Rogelj et al., 2018[39])– makes it difficult to know which represent a realistic and achievable set of energy system transformation pathways. Improvements to modelling are likely to make the models better at representing real-world energy system transformation; however, limitations are likely to remain in the degree to which these models can represent the full range of plausible futures.

Complementary approaches are available and, generally, fall into three groups: (1) qualitative methods, which apply subjectivity and creativity to understand future possibilities, using techniques such as brainstorming, workshops, surveys, expert panels and even science fiction analogies; (2) quantitative methods, which use analytical techniques such as trend extrapolations, time series analyses and modelling; and (3) semi-quantitative methods, which apply mathematical methods to quantify the views of experts and commentators (Popper, 2008[40]).

Some of these other foresight methods could be considered as part of a broader portfolio of techniques aimed at better understanding the range of possible low-emission futures, as well as the associated costs, benefits, uncertainties, risks and opportunities. A critical piece of the research and policy-making agenda is how to combine energy systems models and integrated assessment models activities with these other approaches, to produce a more complete – yet still quantifiable – range of future possibilities to inform today's actions.

In some countries, dedicated foresight units or teams within governments already feed their insights into decision making: Policy Horizons Canada (Canada), the National Institution for Transforming India NITI Aayog (India), the National Institute of Science and Technology Policy (Japan) and the Centre for Strategic Futures (Singapore) are good examples. In Finland, a more diffuse model has emerged with several actors across ministries and the private sector contributing to foresight outputs such as the Government Report on the Future, which is published once during each electoral period (Prime Minister's Office of Finland[41]). Governments have not yet employed these units to inform future iterations of long-term low-emission development strategies as the first ones were communicated to the UNFCCC only in 2016, but such capacity presents an opportunity to enhance the planning process.

Incorporate uncertainty into decision making for resilience

Governments can include the management of climate risks in the specifications and procurement policy for publicly funded infrastructure using emerging decision-making strategies for infrastructure that incorporate uncertainty. While most of the global climate change trends are clear, at the local level some uncertainties represent a cost in themselves, as there is the risk of preparing for a future that fails to materialise. Preparing for the "wrong" future can even be more costly than doing nothing: a study of hydropower in the Zambezi basin found that doing nothing could lead to a loss of 18% of baseline revenues, but the wrong adaptation strategy could cost 30% of baseline revenues (Cervigni et al., 2015[42]).

Flexible, adaptive and proportionate approaches to infrastructure resilience can reduce the costs of building climate resilience given uncertainty about the future. Despite promising high-profile cases of innovative approaches in use (see Box 2.7), the use of formal techniques for decision making under uncertainty remains limited. Even within OECD countries, usage appears limited outside large infrastructure projects: for example, an analysis of 44 local adaptation plans in the United States found that three-quarters of those plans identified uncertainty as an issue, but none of them used formal techniques for decision making under uncertainty (Stults and Larsen, 2018[43]).

Box 2.7. **Foresight techniques in infrastructure planning**

- The **Colorado River Basin** provides water for 30 million people and is increasingly under pressure from growing demand and changing hydrology. Robust Decision Making was used to identify the main drivers of vulnerability and develop portfolios of options for managing supply and demand. The approach was dynamic, identifying the actions that needed to be taken in the near term and those that could be implemented depending on circumstances.
- The **Delta Programme** is responsible for protecting the Netherlands against flood risk and ensuring freshwater supplies. Annual investment is EUR 1 billion per year, split between new investments (60%) and operational expenditures (40%). An approach called "Adaptive Delta Management" has been adopted, which provides a long-term and flexible approach to managing water risks. The analytical tool "Dynamic Adaptive Policy Pathways" has been used to analyse the implications of different choices over time.
- The **Thames Estuary 2100** project was undertaken by the Environment Agency to ensure that London was protected against flooding throughout the 21st century. One of the main decisions was if, and when, to upgrade or replace the Thames Barrier, at a cost of GBP 1.6–5.3 billion. The strategy looked at a broad range of potential outcomes in 2100 and then worked backwards to see which sets of measures would be needed over time to manage those risks. This was combined with the identification and monitoring of decision-points to develop flexible approaches over time.

Sources: Groves, D. et al. (2013[44]), "Adapting to a Changing Colorado River", RAND Corporation; Haasnoot, M. et al. (2013[45]), "Dynamic adaptive policy pathways: A method for crafting robust decisions for a deeply uncertain world", *Global Environmental Change*, 23/2; Ranger, N., T. Reeder and J. Lowe (2013[46]), "Addressing 'deep' uncertainty over long-term climate in major infrastructure projects: four innovations of the Thames Estuary 2100 Project", *EURO Journal on Decision Processes*, 1/3-4.

Notes

1. Its membership currently includes 27 countries (both advanced and developing economies), 15 cities, 17 subnational governments and 192 companies.
2. Launched at COP22 in Marrakesh, the NDC Partnership is a coalition of countries and institutions working to mobilise support and achieve ambitious climate goals while enhancing sustainable development: *https://ndcpartnership.org*
3. According to the 2016 (pg. 12) and 2017 (pg. 13) Joint Reports on MDB Climate Finance. MDBs use a common method for tracking adaptation finance, which identifies adaptation activities within broader development operations carried out in response to perceived or expected climate impacts.

References

2050 Pathways Platform (2017), *2050 Pathways: A Handbook*, *http://www.2050pathways.org/wp-content/uploads/2017/09/2050Pathways-Handbook-1.pdf.* [10]

2050 Pathways Platform (2017), *Why Develop 2050 Pathways?*, 2050 Pathways Platform, *https://www.2050pathways.org/wp-content/uploads/2017/09/Whydevelop2050Pathways.pdf* (accessed on 05 July 2018). [17]

Altieri, K. et al. (2015), *Pathways to Deep Decarbonization in South Africa*, SDSN - IDDRI, *http://deepdecarbonization.org/wp-content/uploads/2015/09/DDPP_ZAF.pdf* (accessed on 05 July 2018). [13]

Cervigni, R. et al. (2015), *Enhancing the Climate Resilience of Africa's Infrastructure: The Power and Water Sectors*, World Bank, Washington, DC, *http://dx.doi.org/10.1596/978-1-4648-0466-3.* [42]

ClimateWorks Australia (2017), *Taking the long view: Why a long term approach for the developing world is critical to achieving sustainable development goals and climate safety*, ClimateWorks Australia, *https://climateworksaustralia.org/sites/default/files/documents/publications/cwa_long_view_issues_paper_0.pdf* (accessed on 19 July 2018). [18]

Dow (2017), *2017 Sustainability Report*, Dow Chemical Company, Midland, Michigan, *https://www.dow.com/en-us/science-and-sustainability/highlights-and-reporting* (accessed on 17 October 2018). [27]

EIA (2017), *Hurricane Irma cut power to nearly two-thirds of Florida's electricity customers*, US Energy Information Administration (EIA) Web Portal, *https://www.eia.gov/todayinenergy/detail.php?id=32992* (accessed on 25 October 2018). [22]

EU High-Level Expert Group on Sustainable Finance (2018), *Financing a Sustainable European Economy: Final Report*, European Commission, *https://ec.europa.eu/info/sites/info/files/180131-sustainable-finance-final-report_en.pdf* (accessed on 05 July 2018). [20]

FAO (2018), *The Future of Food and Agriculture: Alternative Pathways to 2050*, Food and Agriculture Organisation (FAO), Rome, *http://www.fao.org/3/I8429EN/i8429en.pdf* (accessed on 24 October 2018). [6]

Gambhir, A. et al. (2017), "Assessing the Feasibility of Global Long-Term Mitigation Scenarios", *Energies*, Vol. 10/1, p. 89, *http://dx.doi.org/10.3390/en10010089.* [36]

Griscom, B. et al. (2017), "Natural climate solutions", *Proceedings of the National Academy of Sciences of the United States of America*, Vol. 114/44, pp. 11645-11650, *http://dx.doi.org/10.1073/pnas.1710465114.* [31]

Groves, D. et al. (2013), *Adapting to a Changing Colorado River*, *https://www.rand.org/pubs/research_reports/RR242.html.* [44]

Haasnoot, M. et al. (2013), "Dynamic adaptive policy pathways: A method for crafting robust decisions for a deeply uncertain world", *Global Environmental Change*, Vol. 23/2, pp. 485-498, *http://dx.doi.org/10.1016/J.GLOENVCHA.2012.12.006.* [45]

Hallegatte, S., J. Rentschler and B. Walsh (2018), *Building Back Better: Achieving Resilience through Stronger, Faster, and More Inclusive Post-Disaster Reconstruction*, World Bank Group, Washington, DC, *http://hdl.handle.net/10986/29867* (accessed on 27 July 2018). [23]

IEA (2018), *World Energy Investment 2018*, International Energy Agency, *https://www.iea.org/wei2018/.* [4]

IPCC (2018), *Global Warming of 1.5 degrees C*, Intergovernmental Panel on Climate Change, Geneva, *http://www.ipcc.ch/report/sr15/.* [1]

IPCC (2014), *Climate Change 2014: Mitigation of Climate Change: Working Group III Contribution to the Fifth Assessment Report of the Intergovernmental Panel on Climate Change*, Cambridge University Press, *http://www.cambridge.org* (accessed on 22 July 2018). [34]

IPCC (2007), *Climate Change 2007: Mitigation of Climate Change*, Cambridge University Press, *https://www.ipcc.ch/pdf/assessment-report/ar4/wg3/ar4_wg3_full_report.pdf* (accessed on 22 July 2018). [33]

IPCC (2001), *Climate Change 2001: The Scientific Basis*, Intergovernmental Panel on Climate Change, *https://www.ipcc.ch/ipccreports/tar/wg1/pdf/WGI_TAR_full_report.pdf* (accessed on 22 July 2018). [32]

ITF (2017), "Strategic Infrastructure Planning: International Best Practice", *International Transport Forum Policy Papers*, No. 29, OECD Publishing, Paris, *http://dx.doi.org/10.1787/4142787d-en.* [15]

Jones, H., D. Hole and E. Zavaleta (2012), "Harnessing nature to help people adapt to climate change", *Nature Climate Change*, Vol. 2/7, pp. 504-509, *http://dx.doi.org/10.1038/nclimate1463.* [25]

Liu, Q. et al. (2015), *Deep Decarbonization Pathways to in China*, *http://deepdecarbonization.org/wp-content/uploads/2015/09/DDPP_CHN.pdf* (accessed on 11 October 2018). [11]

Nassiry, D., S. Nakhooda and S. Barnard (2016), *Finding the Pipeline: Project Preparation for Sustainable Infrastructure*, Overseas Development Institute (ODI) & New Climate Economy, *http://newclimateeconomy.report/workingpapers/wp-content/uploads/sites/5/2016/11/Finding-the-Pipeline.pdf.* [8]

OECD (2018), *Capital Budgeting and Infrastructure Survey 2018 (forthcoming)*, OECD Publishing, Paris. [14]

OECD (2018), *Developing Robust Project Pipelines for Low-Carbon Infrastructure (forthcoming)*, OECD Publishing, Paris. [16]

OECD (2018), *Rethinking Urban Sprawl: Moving Towards Sustainable Cities*, OECD Publishing, Paris, *http://dx.doi.org/10.1787/9789264189881-en.* [7]

OECD (2017), *Investing in Climate, Investing in Growth*, OECD Publishing, Paris, *http://dx.doi.org/10.1787/9789264273528-en.* [3]

OECD (2016), *Green Investment Banks: Scaling up Private Investment in Low-carbon, Climate-resilient Infrastructure*, Green Finance and Investment, OECD Publishing, Paris, *http://dx.doi.org/10.1787/9789264245129-en.* [21]

Palacin, R. (2016), "Hyperloop, the Electrification of Mobility, and the Future of Rail Travel", *IEEE Electrification Magazine*, September 2016, Institute of Electrical and Electronics Engineers (IEEE), *https://doi.org/10.1109/MELE.2016.2584918.* [38]

Popper, R. (2008), "Foresight methodology", in Georghiou, L. (ed.), *The Handbook of Technology Foresight: Concepts and Practice*, Edward Elgar Publishing. [40]

Prime Minister's Office of Finland (n.d.), *Government report on the future*, *https://vnk.fi/en/government-report-on-the-future* (accessed on 04 September 2018). [41]

Ranger, N., T. Reeder and J. Lowe (2013), "Addressing 'deep' uncertainty over long-term climate in major infrastructure projects: four innovations of the Thames Estuary 2100 Project", *EURO Journal on Decision Processes*, Vol. 1/3-4, pp. 233-262, *http://dx.doi.org/10.1007/s40070-013-0014-5.* [46]

Riahi, K. et al. (2015), "Locked into Copenhagen pledges — Implications of short-term emission targets for the cost and feasibility of long-term climate goals", *Technological Forecasting and Social Change*, Vol. 90, pp. 8-23, *http://dx.doi.org/10.1016/J.TECHFORE.2013.09.016.* [37]

Rogelj, J. et al. (2013), "Probabilistic cost estimates for climate change mitigation", *Nature*, Vol. 493/7430, pp. 79-83, *http://dx.doi.org/10.1038/nature11787.* [35]

Rogelj, J. et al. (2018), "Scenarios towards limiting global mean temperature increase below 1.5 °C", *Nature Climate Change*, Vol. 8/4, pp. 325-332, *http://dx.doi.org/10.1038/s41558-018-0091-3.* [39]

Röttgers, D. and B. Anderson (2018), "Drivers and barriers to the decarbonisation of the electricity sector (forthcoming)", *OECD Environment Working Papers*, OECD Publishing, Paris, *http://dx.doi.org/10.1787/19970900.* [9]

Shearer, C. et al. (2018), *Boom and Bust 2018: Tracking the Global Coal Plant Pipeline*, CoalSwarm, Sierra Club & Greenpeace, *https://endcoal.org/wp-content/uploads/2018/03/BoomAndBust_2018_r4.pdf* (accessed on 11 September 2018). [5]

Smith, P. et al. (2014), "Agriculture, Forestry and Other Land Use (AFOLU)", in Edenhofer, O. et al. (eds.), *Climate Change 2014: Mitigation of Climate Change*, Cambridge University Press, Cambridge, United Kingdom and New York, NY, USA, *http://www.ipcc.ch/pdf/assessment-report/ar5/wg3/ipcc_wg3_ar5_chapter11.pdf* (accessed on 27 July 2018). [30]

Stults, M. and L. Larsen (2018), "Tackling Uncertainty in US Local Climate Adaptation Planning", *Journal of Planning Education and Research*, pp. 1-16, *http://dx.doi.org/10.1177/0739456X18769134*. [43]

Talberth, J. et al. (2012), "Insights from the Field: Forests for Water", *Southern Forests for the Future Incentives Series*, No. 9, World Resources Institute, Washington, DC, *https://www.wri.org/publication/insights-field-forests-water*. [26]

The Nature Conservancy (2018), *Launch of the Coastal Zone Management Trust*, The Nature Conservancy, Quintana Roo, *https://thought-leadership-production.s3.amazonaws.com/2018/03/08/14/23/46/1ac3a4be-11d2-4651-9d98-50326d81e1b8/TNC_Mexico_Coastal ManagementTrust_Factsheet.pdf* (accessed on 17 October 2018). [28]

UN Environment (2018), *Greening the Belt and Road Initiative (forthcoming)*, UN Environment. [19]

UNFCCC (n.d.), *Communication of long-term strategies*, *https://unfccc.int/process/the-paris-agreement/long-term-strategies* (accessed on 17 October 2018). [2]

Vallejo, L. and M. Mullan (2017), "Climate-resilient infrastructure: Getting the policies right", *OECD Environment Working Papers*, No. 121, OECD Publishing, Paris, *https://doi.org/10.1787/19970900*. [24]

Waisman, H. et al. (2015), *Pathways to Deep Decarbonization*, IDDRI, *https://www.iddri.org/sites/default/files/import/publications/ddpp_2015synthetisreport.pdf* (accessed on 03 July 2018). [12]

World Bank (2017), *Implementing nature-based flood protection Principles and implementation guidance*, World Bank, *https://openknowledge.worldbank.org/handle/10986/28837*. [29]

Financing Climate Futures
Rethinking Infrastructure

Chapter 3

Unleash innovation to accelerate the transition

Innovation is critical for the economic transformation required to address climate change. The rate and direction of innovation will, to a large extent, determine the economic cost and therefore the likelihood of achieving the Paris Agreement's mitigation and adaptation goals. This chapter examines current trends in innovation. It highlights the barriers and opportunities for accelerating the deployment of technologies, business models and services that support the transition to a low-emission, resilient future. The chapter outlines four priority actions for scaling up climate solutions: deploy targeted innovation policies to create and shape markets for climate innovations, scale up public investment in research and development (R&D), overcome financial barriers to demonstration and early-stage commercialisation to bring existing technologies to scale, and promote international technology diffusion to ensure that innovation benefits all.

Key messages

To deliver the economic transformation required to address climate change, governments must accelerate the deployment of existing technologies, business models and services, and swiftly move the next generation of climate solutions from the lab to the market. To scale up climate solutions, governments should:

- Deploy targeted innovation policies to create and shape markets for climate innovations.
- Scale up public investment in research and development to create the next generation of climate solutions.
- Overcome the financial barriers to demonstration and early-stage commercialisation to bring existing technologies to scale.
- Promote international technology diffusion to ensure that innovation benefits all.

Why is innovation transformative?

Innovation – the creation and diffusion of new products, processes and methods – is fundamental to the economic transformation required to address climate change. The rate and direction of innovation will, to a large extent, determine the economic cost and therefore the likelihood of achieving the Paris Agreement's mitigation and adaptation goals.

The world requires a radical change in the mix of technologies that underpin the production and consumption of goods and services. The IPCC Special Report on the impacts of global warming of 1.5°C finds that:

> *Pathways limiting global warming to 1.5°C with no or limited overshoot would require rapid and far-reaching transitions in energy, land, urban and infrastructure (including transport and buildings), and industrial systems [...]. The systems transitions consistent with adapting to and limiting global warming to 1.5°C include the widespread adoption of new and possibly disruptive technologies and practices and enhanced climate-driven innovation* (IPCC, 2018[1]).

Opportunities for low-emission innovations are economy-wide, and include: technologies for renewable energy, energy storage and smart grids; energy-efficient lighting, heating and cooling in buildings; electric, hybrid and fuel-efficient vehicles; more efficient crop varieties, vaccines to inhibit methane production by ruminants and laboratory-grown meat; and carbon capture, storage and use technologies. New technologies such as permeable materials for pavements and roads, drought-resilient crops and improved irrigation schemes could also help populations adapt to climate impacts.

Innovation is not only about the development and diffusion of new and disruptive technologies. It is just as much about institutional and organisational changes, and new services and business models (e.g. energy-as-a-service platforms, electric car sharing, circular supply models), all of which can help drive the systemic changes needed in production and consumption for the transition towards a low-emission, resilient future. Technological and non-technological innovations can work in tandem to significantly reduce the demand for infrastructure services and open up new and more cost-effective pathways to achieve the goals of the Paris Agreement.

What is the state of play?

The development of technologies for climate change mitigation and adaptation has increased rapidly since the beginning of the century. Globally, the number of patented inventions related to climate change mitigation in buildings, transport and energy generation tripled between 2000 and 2010. However, inventive activity has been slowing across all major environment-related domains since 2011, both in absolute terms and as a share of total inventions (OECD, 2017[2]). This might partly be a result of the recent fall in energy prices, which makes the value of future energy savings smaller, as well as the continued uncertainty over national and global climate policies.

However, there has been some progress in the diffusion of low-emission technologies. Renewable energy sources such as solar and wind are now cost-competitive with conventional sources of electricity in some markets and are being quickly brought to scale (IEA, 2017[3]). Progress has also been made across other sectors such as transport, where there have been improvements in vehicle efficiency and a doubling of electric car sales between 2014 and 2017 (IEA, 2018[4]). In forestry and agriculture, satellite imagery has revolutionised data collection and monitoring of deforestation, helping to inform policy making and enhance enforcement efforts.

Many of the emerging innovations have their roots in the digital revolution. Digital technologies are facilitating investment and citizen engagement in renewable energy and other sustainable development projects enabling more decentralised and flexible energy systems, and increasing energy efficiency (see Box 3.1). For example, smart charging technologies for electric vehicles are helping address intermittency in renewable energy supply, while smart meters are changing energy consumption patterns in homes and businesses.

Despite pockets of progress, the current level of innovation falls short of what is needed to reach the 2°C goal, let alone move towards 1.5°C, with severe implications for human health and well-being, biodiversity and economic growth. Of 38 clean-energy technologies included in the IEA's Sustainable Development Scenario in their World Energy Outlook (which is consistent with the 2°C goal), only four are on track to penetrate markets sufficiently: solar photovoltaic, lighting, data centres and networks, and electric vehicles. The majority of technologies need more progress, and a quarter are classified as "not on track", including carbon capture and storage, concentrating solar power and geothermal and ocean technologies (IEA, 2018[4]).

What are the barriers and opportunities for change?

To increase the likelihood and reduce the cost of achieving and adapting to the 1.5°C or 2°C goals, the world must accelerate the deployment of existing innovations in technology, business models and services, and swiftly move the next generation of climate solutions from the lab to the market. These innovations need to be adopted as widely as possible to ensure shared prosperity and an inclusive transition to a low-emission and resilient future. As no single government has all the technological, scientific, financial and other resources needed to address climate change, it is important that strong national policies for innovation are accompanied by effective international co-operation in the development and diffusion of innovations.

Advanced, emerging and developing economies face different challenges and opportunities in delivering climate solutions. However, there are four principal barriers to innovation that they all must overcome. First, markets undersupply innovation because of the positive externalities associated with the generation and diffusion of knowledge (i.e. firms do not capture all the benefits of their innovations). Second, when firms and households do not have to pay for environmental services or the costs of pollution, the demand for green innovation is limited and the incentives for companies to invest are lower. Third, financing of the more radical types of innovation that could potentially be introduced by new market participants is constrained by information asymmetries, which can be exacerbated if there is uncertainty concerning future policy settings. Fourth, the international dissemination of climate technologies can be undermined by trade barriers and a lack of country capacity to adopt, adapt and deploy new technologies.

Innovation is not only critical for addressing climate change; it lays the foundation for new businesses, new jobs and productivity growth and it can help drive progress towards other Sustainable Development Goals (SDGs). To reap the full benefits of innovation, governments need to have the foresight and flexibility to take advantage of new technologies and opportunities, such as the digital revolution, and be prepared to break dependencies on institutions and technologies with which they are familiar.

Box 3.1. **Harnessing digital finance to engage citizens in sustainable development**

Digital finance encompasses a broad range of new software, customer interaction tools, financial products and business models. It presents new opportunities for raising capital, enhancing transparency and access to information, and making market mechanisms more inclusive. For example, new online platforms can aggregate global data on isolated investment opportunities, cutting the number of intermediaries between investors and project holders. Blockchain technologies can serve to enhance market transparency by offering "smart contracts" and keeping an immutable record of transactions made (see Box 5.3). The examples below highlight how online platforms, mobile phone applications and other digital technologies are engaging and empowering citizen-consumers.

Leveraging mobile phone technology

M-Pesa is a mobile phone-based service that enables easy deposit, withdrawal and transfer of money. Since its launch in 2007 in Kenya and Tanzania, it has enjoyed great success and spread to other developing countries. It has also enabled further innovation in the form of the M-Kopa, through which customers pay a deposit for a solar kit through M-Pesa as well as a daily rent for 12 months, at which point they become the owner of the device. In 2014, just two years after its launch, M-Kopa secured a USD 10 million (860 million Kenyan shillings) commercial-grade syndicated debt facility fronted by the Commercial Bank of Africa (CBA), which enabled it to extend its operations. To date, M-Kopa has raised USD 45 million in total equity funding and debt financing, and has connected 600 000 customers to affordable solar power. Similar pay-as-you-go (PAYG) solar solutions have been deployed across Africa, Asia and Latin America, for example Simpa Networks in India and Quetsol in Guatemala. These companies have the potential to revolutionise the low-income energy sector.

The latest arrival on the scene is M-Akiba, a retail bond issued by the Government of Kenya through which citizens have the opportunity to invest directly in infrastructure development projects. A low minimum level of investment (approximately USD 30 or 3 000 Kenyan shillings) offers them an affordable savings product, with 10% per annum fixed returns over three years comparable to peer financial saving products. The government hopes to borrow approximately USD 50 million (5 billion Kenyan shillings) through the bond. To date, it has raised approximately USD 2.4 million (247.75 million Kenyan shillings), and while it is still small scale today, M-Akiba together with M-Kopa and M-Pesa have already shown the potential of digital finance to catalyse broader public participation in sustainable development projects and empower citizens to make informed and sustainable decisions.

Box 3.1. **Harnessing digital finance to engage citizens in sustainable development** *(cont.)*

Matchmaking

Motif Investing is an online platform that relies on algorithms to detect and offer investment products, including in sustainability and infrastructure (e.g. solar, wind, electrical vehicles and biofuels). It specifically targets younger investors interested in low-fee impactful investments that are aligned with their environmental values, but also engages in business-to-business activities, for example with Goldman Sachs and JP Morgan Chase. This means that these large banks can offer portfolios that include sustainability investments without having to build them in-house, or having to compete for the next generation of investors.

Another example is the Canadian platform Convergence Finance, which hosts an online database that enables a quick and easy search for credible deals in emerging economies. This simplifies and shortens screening processes and broadens the pool of potential investors. A dedicated programme, called 'Design Funding', also offers project proponents support to run feasibility studies and to access proof-of-concept funding. As of May 2018, Convergence Finance had awarded USD 5 million of grants to 15 projects, thereby mobilising USD 110 million. Convergence Finance has funded large projects such as the establishment of a Climate Finance Facility in partnership with the Development Bank of Southern Africa (DBSA), the Coalition for Green Capital (CGC) and ClimateWorks Foundation. The facility will focus climate-friendly infrastructure projects in countries of the Southern African Development Community.

Crowdfunding

LittleBigMoney is a Colombian crowdfunding platform for social and environmental projects. The platform offers a registry of available projects and an online tool to finance them. Interactive features, such as video presentations of the projects, provide a personalised experience to investors. To date, LittleBigMoney has facilitated over 4 000 projects, bringing together more than 1 600 stakeholders, and mobilised almost 500 million Colombian pesos (USD 170 000).

Digitalisation presents transformative opportunities to empower citizens and drive the low-emission transition, but its possible unintended consequences are still poorly understood. Digital technologies consume large amounts of electricity, which could offset the energy efficiency gains it can deliver. Digitalisation of the energy sector also renders systems more vulnerable to cyber attacks, raises concerns about data privacy, and can create significant changes in work patterns, tasks and skills. All of these potential issues need to be prepared for and addressed with tailored policies.

Nonetheless, there appears to be widespread consensus on the importance of further exploring the potential for digital finance to advance sustainable finance, as recognised by the G20 under Argentina's Presidency, and by the launch of a Task Force on Digital Financing for the Sustainable Development Goals by the UN Secretary-General in 2018.

Source: UN Environment (2018[5]), Digital Finance and Citizen Action in Financing the Future of Climate-Smart Infrastructure (forthcoming), *Financing Climate Futures Case Studies*.

3.1. Deploy targeted innovation policies to create and shape markets for climate innovations

Getting the basics right: the enabling environment for climate innovations

A sound enabling environment for innovation – e.g. well-aligned tax, competition, education, science, trade and investment policies – and a strong environmental policy framework must underpin efforts to scale up climate mitigation and adaptation innovation (OECD, 2015[6]; Ang, Röttgers and Burli, 2017[7]). Governments can help increase investor confidence and ensure that innovation activity supports rather than undermines the low-emission transition by setting a clear and stable policy signal through long-term low-emission development strategies (see Chapter 2) and carbon pricing. For example, the introduction of the European Union emissions trading system induced regulated companies to file 30% more patents in low-carbon technologies (Calel and Dechezleprêtre, 2016[8]). However, the price of carbon emissions globally is still extremely low (OECD, 2018[9])(see Chapter 4). Increasing the price on carbon would help catalyse private sector innovation in a cost-efficient manner, without burdening (and possibly even replenishing) public budgets. It would also incentivise behavioural responses by consumers, triggering additional energy savings.

A strong enabling environment for innovation is a necessary but not a sufficient condition for the transformation. To deliver transformative change, governments must also adopt a suite of demand- and supply-side innovation policies and finance measures that are tailored to the climate challenge.

Moving to the next frontier: mission-oriented programmes

One way governments can set the direction of innovation is by adopting mission-oriented programmes. Mission-oriented programmes align policies, public R&D programmes and public-private collaboration to overcome a concrete problem. This in turn helps to address a broader societal challenge or "wicked problem" – one that is complex, systemic, interconnected and urgent – such as climate change, environmental degradation and public health challenges (Box 3.2). At the core of the mission-oriented approach is the understanding that governments must not only correct market failures, but also actively drive and direct innovation by co-creating and co-shaping markets (Foray, Mowery and Nelson, 2012[10]; Mazzucato, 2017[11]).

Strengthening the market pull for climate innovations: demand-side policies

In the last decade, increasing attention has been paid to the role of demand-side policies for innovation to supplement the more traditional supply-side policies (e.g. R&D support). Demand-side policies can help direct resources and capabilities by creating or strengthening the market pull for climate innovations. In general, governments should emphasise competition and technology neutrality, rather than supporting specific technologies and solutions. However, judicious use of more technology-specific measures may be required to overcome the barriers facing low-emission technologies and drive transformative rather than incremental innovation. Feed-in-tariffs (FITs), for example, were instrumental in bringing wind power in Denmark and Germany to full commercialisation at a time when the technology was not yet competitive (OECD, 2011[18]).

National and subnational regulations or performance standards have also demonstrated their effectiveness in encouraging more innovation. These include energy-efficient building codes or renewable portfolio standards that require electricity providers to include a minimum share of clean energy in their output mix (e.g. California Renewables Portfolio Standard) (Rozenberg, Vogt-Schilb and Hallegatte, 2014[19]). However, these instruments tend to benefit technologies that are closer to market. This points to the need for a broad policy mix that includes both technology-specific and technology-neutral measures, regulatory and economic instruments, and direct R&D funding for technologies that are further from the market.

National and subnational public procurement can also be used to create market pull for climate innovations. By introducing climate-related criteria in procurement decisions, public procurement can bring low-emission solutions to market and trigger industrial and business model innovation through the creation of lead markets (Baron, 2017[20]). A number of governments have adopted sustainable public procurement criteria and practices, such as tenders with lifecycle costing that incorporates the costs of emissions in value-for-money assessments, and market dialogues to help procurers and potential suppliers to formulate innovative tenders (OECD, 2017[21]). Like regulations and standards, procurement can spur innovation without engaging new spending.

Box 3.2. **Mission-oriented innovation to drive a green, low-emission transition**

Germany – Energiewende (energy transition)

The German *Energiewende* is a mission-oriented programme aimed at creating a low-carbon energy system, while at the same time phasing out nuclear power by 2022. The programme is governed by the Federal Ministry for Economic Affairs and Energy, in close interaction with regional governments and private entities. Households and energy co-operatives own a large share of the renewable energy systems, which has increased flexibility and fostered public acceptance: 90% of citizens believe the programme to be vital (O'Donnell and Gruenig, 2016[12]; Kuittinen and Velte, 2018[13]). The *Energiewende* is supported by a combination of tax incentives (e.g. to incentivise the retro-fitting of buildings), government-funded research programmes and low-interest loans from the state investment bank (KfW Group), for renewable energy and energy efficiency investments (Kuittinen and Velte, 2018[13]). Public finance has leveraged significant private investments in energy retrofits and renewable energy installations, closing the gap between public-sector involvement and the real costs of the *Energiewende* (O'Donnell and Gruenig, 2016[12]).

China – New Electric Vehicles

China's first targeted policy to promote New Electric Vehicles (NEVs) was launched in 2001 by the Ministry of Science and Technology. In the years to follow, the policy was extended and a range of ministries – for example the National Development and Reform Commission, the Ministry of Industry and Information Technology and the Ministry of Finance – as well as regional governments were engaged. The aim is to have five million NEVs on the road by 2020, and at least one in every five cars sold in China to be a new energy model by 2025. Both demand- and supply-side policies are being deployed to reach these goals, including: R&D projects; support for commercialisation; tax credits and fiscal rewards for purchasing NEVs; tighter regulations on combustion engine cars; public procurement and setting standards. While China has become the largest electric car market in the world, it does not appear to be on track to reach its mission goals by 2020 and 2025 (OECD, 2014[14]; Pelkonen, 2018[15]).

Belgium – Circular Flanders

Circular Flanders is a multi-stakeholder platform consisting of authorities, companies, non-profit organisations, civil society and academics with the mission to create circular economies for materials, energy, water and food in the Belgian region of Flanders. A change of thinking in the beginning of the century led to the creation of a variety of initiatives related to the circular economy. *Circular Flanders* was launched in 2017, integrating three of these: Plan C, a circular economy hub; SuMMa, a policy research institute; and Agenda 2020, a list of 45 concrete projects. The programme links with the Flemish government's Vision 2050, which establishes the circular economy as one of seven "transition priorities". While the main governing body of *Circular Flanders* is the Public Waste Agency, the transition priority is under the joint responsibility of the Ministry of Environment and the Ministry for Economy and Innovation. The program has six core activities: creating a network; offering financial support; sharing knowledge; developing policies; stimulating directed innovation; and scaling up best practices. It has been estimated that investment in the circular economy could cut materials expenses by 2-3.5% of GDP, as well as create 27 000 new jobs in Flanders. However, it is difficult to quantify outputs and outcomes to date as no overall targets have been set and no indicators exist to monitor the initiative (Tuerk and Bird, 2018[16]; Circular Flanders, 2017[17]).

A less apparent demand-side policy that can promote innovation is standardisation. If standardisation occurs too early, it may shut out better technologies; if it occurs too late, the costs of transition may prevent diffusion of non-compliant innovations. However, if employed with care, standardisation can help create critical mass to benefit from economies of scale. An example of standardisation in practice is charging infrastructure for electric vehicles. Standards for physical plugs, as well as for payment and power supply could create a competitive market, while also ensuring consumer convenience. The EU standardised the electric plug used for normal alternating current (AC) charging in 2014, but competing systems exist for the more recent direct current (DC) fast charging and wireless charging technology. If standards are not designed with flexibility, they can be outpaced by technological developments.

Consumers can also catalyse and influence the direction of innovation. Governments can empower consumers by deploying policies that counter inertia and scepticism about new goods and services (OECD, 2011[22]). Monetary or price-based incentives such as demand subsidies or tax allowances can encourage risk-averse consumers to buy innovative new products. For example, Belgium's Walloon Social Credit Society (SWCS) offers advantageous loans to low-income households under its "Ecopack" scheme. These support the adoption of energy efficiency measures: installing heat pumps, photovoltaic panels, solar water-heaters and pellet stoves; or insulating roofs, walls and floors (Société Wallonne du Crédit Social[23]). Information and awareness campaigns can also be used to influence consumer preferences and behaviour, where there may be information failures.

3.2. Deliver and scale up support for research and development of climate solutions

Research is the foundation of future innovation, but tends to be under-supplied by the private sector due to its long time horizon and the uncertainties surrounding the future commercial viability of any resulting technologies. Governments can help scale up R&D from private firms and universities through direct funding in the form of loans and grants, or through fiscal incentives, such as tax credits. Aligning R&D subsidies for fossil fuel research with low- and net-zero emissions goals is equally important.

Realising the full potential of innovation to drive the transition to a low-emission economy will require much greater levels of public investment in R&D. While estimates of the funding gap vary, there is a broad consensus that public investment in low-emission R&D would have to at least double to reach the goals of the Paris Agreement (Dechezleprêtre, Martin and Bassi, 2016[24]). There are positive signs that governments are starting to respond to this need, at least for certain sectors. The IEA (2018[25])indicates that public innovation investment in clean energy technologies increased by 13% in 2017 to USD 22 billion, breaking a streak of declines and stagnation over several years. Furthermore, through the international initiative "Mission Innovation", 23 countries and the European Union have pledged to double their clean energy R&D spending by 2021 to address climate change, make clean energy affordable and create new jobs and commercial opportunities. If the pledge is achieved, the combined annual R&D investment from these countries will rise to approximately USD 30 billion per year (Mission Innovation, 2018[26]).

Public research through government research institutes and laboratories has an important role to play in linking basic and applied research. In addition to targeting technological progress, public research should explore socioeconomic and political aspects that could help deliver systemic changes in production and consumption practices, habits and behaviour or that could influence the acceptance and adoption of new technologies. The French Environment and Energy Management Agency's Strategic Roadmap for Smart Electricity Systems, for instance, identifies research priorities concerning economic and regulatory conditions (e.g. developing innovative business models to support the integration of energy storage systems), and human and social sciences (e.g. identifying and analysing the governance processes needed for innovations to spread), in addition to technological research priorities.

Box 3.3. **Collaborative approaches to R&D**

National multi-stakeholder collaboration for R&D

The SunShot Initiative

The US Department of Energy's Sunshot Initiative strives to make solar energy cost competitive by the end of the decade. SunShot awards partial funding for R&D projects to the best bids from companies, universities, state and local governments, non-profit organisations and national laboratories. The programme met its 2020 target of decreasing utility-scale solar energy cost from USD 0.28/kWh to USD 0.06/kWh three years earlier than expected. Similarly, the price of residential solar power dropped from USD 0.52 in 2010 to USD 0.16 in 2017, and from USD 0.40 to USD 0.11 for commercial use (US Department of Energy[28]).

European Institute of Innovation and Technology's KIC

With more than 300 partners from education, research, business and government, the European Institute of Innovation and Technology's Climate-KIC is the EU's largest and most extensive public-private partnership to accelerate the transition to a net-zero emissions economy. Operating from 13 centres, the initiative takes a broad approach by offering educational programs, supporting research and development, as well as fostering entrepreneurship (Climate-KIC[29]).

International collaboration for R&D

US-China Clean Energy Research Center

The US-China Clean Energy Research Center aims to generate a diversified energy supply and accelerate the transition to an efficient and low-emission economy, while delivering economic and environmental benefits to both countries. It is supported by public and private funding of at least USD 250 million over five years (2016-2020) and focuses on five technical tracks, including energy efficiency, water and energy technologies and clean vehicles. Each research consortium has a joint work plan and technology management plan, as part of a broader intellectual property framework (Energetics Incorporated, 2018[30]).

Strengthening International Cooperation on Climate Change Research (SINCERE)

SINCERE is a project by the European Union running from 2018-2022 with a budget of EUR 2.2 million, which aims to strengthen international climate change research and innovation co-operation involving European countries. SINCERE will involve the business sector and global financial institutions, other key international research as well as policy and societal actors. A particular goal is expanding the existing EU Joint Programme Initiative (JPI) Climate to include Eastern European member countries; another is to set up two flagship actions with Africa and Latin America (European Commission, 2018[31]).

International Energy Agency (IEA) Technology Collaboration Programmes

The IEA's Technology Collaboration Programmes involve over 6 000 experts worldwide who represent nearly 300 public and private organisations located in 55 countries. To date, participants in the programmes have examined around 2 000 energy-related topics, and carried out projects on socioeconomic aspects of technology deployment, research to reduce greenhouse gas emissions, advancing demonstration of innovative energy technologies, contributing to benchmarks and international standards, and sharing information through hundreds of expert stakeholder events (IEA[32]).

Well-designed collaborations between the public and private sectors, across firms, and among academia and national laboratories can help match problem-owners with solution-providers, pool resources, bring together complementary skills and expertise, and lower technology risks and R&D costs (Box 3.3). International co-operation on R&D can also accelerate innovation by enabling larger-scale projects, avoiding duplication and bringing together different skills and expertise. Co-operation can take place in a multilateral context with open participation, in limited-member groups or bilaterally. To ensure that co-operation is successful, care must be taken to balance different mandates and restrictions, and clearly define and co-ordinate management and responsibilities (OECD, 2014[27]).

Bottom-up open innovation strategies can also facilitate the emergence of innovations not prioritised by strategic road-mapping or technology and innovation assessments, and hence help prevent potentially promising innovations from being overlooked. Open innovation strategies can be pursued through challenge-led calls, which utilise prize competitions, crowdsourcing, ideation or open dialogues.

3.3. Overcome the financial barriers to demonstration and early-stage commercialisation

Innovative technologies and solutions emerging from R&D must pass through several stages of validation and refinement before reaching full commercialisation, and will depend on different types of investors and investment instruments along the way. These include angel investors and venture capital funds, corporates and corporate venture capital funds, financial institutions, civil society (e.g. crowdfunding) and philanthropists. Due to information asymmetry and the fragmented nature of investor networks, projects may face a discontinuity of investment and fall into a so-called funding "valley of death". This tends to occur at the demonstration phase (the "technology valley of death") or at early-stage commercialisation (the "commercialisation valley of death") (In, Monk and Levitt, 2017[33]).

Clean energy technologies that require large-scale capital investment, have long development timelines and face high technology risks are particularly vulnerable to funding gaps (Gaddy, Sivaram and O'Sullivan, 2016[34]). Indeed, recent analyses have highlighted the limitations of traditional venture capital (VC) models for funding such innovations. Although VC has played an important role in accelerating the commercialisation of some clean energy technologies, recent investment in clean technology tends to focus on a narrow range of more mature technologies, with energy efficiency and transportation receiving the lion's share (IEA, 2017[35]). This may be due in part to the time and capital constraints of VC investors and the relatively poor risk-return profile of clean energy investments (Gaddy, Sivaram and O'Sullivan, 2016[34]).

While a strong enabling investment environment is fundamental for pulling innovations through the valley of death, there is also a need to diversify and better align the investment vehicles and actors involved at the different stages of innovation, and to improve the allocation of investment risk. Governments can help bridge the valley of death by supporting the expansion of public and private incubators (e.g. Israel's Incubators Centre for Technological Initiative) and accelerators (e.g. Start-Up Chile), and by using public money to fund risky, long-term projects that could have large social benefits but are too early for private-sector investment. The US Department of Energy's Advanced Research Project Agency, for instance, provides researchers with funding, technical assistance and support for market readiness to help them develop new ways to generate, store and use energy.

Low-interest loans, loan guarantees, tax incentives and quasi-equity financing can be deployed to reduce investment risk and attract private sector finance. The European Commission and the European Investment Bank have developed a EUR 150 million programme, InnovFin Energy Demonstration Project, to fill the funding gap for first-of-a-kind demonstration projects for innovative energy technologies in the EU. The programme will provide funding of between EUR 7.5 million and EUR 75 million to large-scale energy demonstration project developers.

Governments can promote and facilitate new partnerships and coalitions to help align investment vehicles and actors, thereby ensuring a continued stream of investment all along the innovation chain from basic research through to deployment of new technologies. For example, the global Breakthrough Energy Coalition and its Breakthrough Energy Ventures funding mechanism bring together patient and risk-tolerant private investors, global corporations and financial institutions with the capital necessary to finance large energy infrastructure projects that emerge under the Mission Innovation initiative.

3.4. Promote international technology diffusion at scale

The wide diffusion of low-emission and climate adaptation innovations is critical for achieving the goals of the Paris Agreement and broader environment and sustainable development objectives. The adoption of strong environmental policies can drive international technology diffusion, as it helps create markets for low-emission innovations and provides firms with incentives to acquire new technologies. However, because technology diffusion takes place primarily through trade, foreign direct investment (FDI) and other market channels, removing tariff and non-tariff barriers to trade in low-emission technologies and manufacturing equipment is fundamental (OECD, 2011[36]). Indeed, Chinese producers became world leaders in photovoltaic panel production through the purchase of manufacturing equipment on the global market (De La Tour, Glachant and Ménière, 2011[37]). The deployment of climate mitigation and adaptation technologies often depends on the availability of specialised services, including those imported from other countries, pointing to the importance of lowering barriers to trade in services.

The extent and effectiveness of technology diffusion are determined not only by markets, but also by the absorptive capacity of recipient countries. The higher the level of domestic human capital, the higher the level of technology transfer as well as the local spillovers from trade and FDI (OECD, 2011[36]). Investing in education, technical extension services, public technology diffusion programmes and demonstrators is therefore important to enhance the ability of the public and private sectors to adopt, adapt and employ the most appropriate technologies. It can also help to facilitate the transition of economies and workers dependent on energy-intensive industries (Box 3.4).

International transfers of low-emission technologies have been primarily between advanced countries. The diffusion of climate change mitigation technologies to and from developing countries – particularly emerging economies – has increased significantly since 1992. In 2016, emerging economies accounted for 29% of the global imports of low-emission equipment goods and 24% of global exports. While emerging economies are better integrated into international technology markets, less developed countries remain largely excluded due to their general isolation and lack of absorptive capacity (Glachant and Dechezleprêtre, 2017[38]). International technology transfer mechanisms and development co-operation have an important role to play in ensuring that innovation benefits a larger number of countries.

International mechanisms have been established to support North-South and South-South technology diffusion, such as the UNFCCC's Technology Mechanism, the South-South Knowledge Exchange under The Energy and Resources Institute, IEA's Collaborative Technology Agreements and the new Technology Facilitation Mechanism established under the 2030 Agenda.

Box 3.4. **Decarbonising energy-intensive industries will be a key challenge to meeting climate objectives**

The industry sector relies heavily on fossil fuels (e.g. iron, steel, cement and chemicals manufacture), which makes its decarbonisation particularly challenging. Between 1990 and 2014, global industrial greenhouse gas emissions rose by 69%, all sectors included, which is three times more than in buildings, power generation and transport. Deep decarbonisation will require simultaneous technology, policy and financing innovations, as well as sector-specific pathways to net-zero emissions in order to ensure businesses' competitiveness is maintained.

Existing technologies and processes can help support the sector's decarbonisation including in: material efficiency and recycling; energy efficiency and heat integration; fuel switching from coal to natural gas; or advanced control, optimisation and improved monitoring practices. However, such technologies and processes will not put energy-intensive industries on track with the 2050 Paris Agreement goals, and there is an urgent need for deploying new technologies that can achieve deep decarbonisation.

Some of these new technologies that can help deliver these changes include:

1. Electrification of heat and high-temperature processes;
2. Fuel switching to sustainable biomass;
3. Advanced waste-heat recovery;
4. Carbon Capture and Storage (CCS); and
5. Other sector-specific process modifications, such as solid-state synthesis for ammonia production, which can potentially fully eliminate CO_2 emissions.

However, such technologies are both capital and risk intensive, and their market uptake will require fostering new skills, knowledge and value chains to support long-term financial viability and competitiveness. Some policy and financing can help achieve this:

- International collaboration on decarbonisation policies and projects is necessary in order to stimulate co-operation among businesses. This can also help prevent relocation of investments from countries subject to environmental laws to less regulated areas of the world, which has been a concern for governments sometimes limiting their decarbonisation efforts.
- At the national level, stable and predictable regulatory frameworks are equally important, in order to maintain market confidence and limit investment risks and higher costs of capital.
- Encouraging companies to consider technologies with longer payback periods than usual is also essential to avoid locking in inefficient technologies.
- Collaborative initiatives with trade associations, peer-to-peer businesses or academia can be particularly effective platforms for sharing and fostering decarbonisation best practices.
- Other well-known policies such as removal of energy subsidies, emission reduction targets, carbon trading, environmental taxes, ear-marked grants, or public procurement tools can help drive decarbonisation further too. An example of such policies is the UK government Renewable Heat Incentive ('RHI'), introduced in 2011, which provides a payment for each unit of renewable high-grade heat generated (e.g. from biomass and biogas) to businesses in the iron, steel, cement, and chemicals sectors – which could cover three quarters of total industrial heat demand in the UK by 2030.

Box 3.4. Decarbonising energy-intensive industries will be a key challenge to meeting climate objectives *(cont.)*

If successful, the decarbonisation of energy-intensive industries may also generate a range of benefits such as new employment opportunities. It may, however, also lead to job destruction and stranded workers. The low-skilled workforce is likely to be the most affected by the transition to low-emission economies, as more qualified employees will capture new opportunities in green technology and innovation more easily. Entire communities of low-skilled workers could be affected by a rapid transition in particular regions where emissions-intensive industries are a dominant employer. In these areas, dedicated resources will need to help workers from declining fossil-fuel industries to ensure they are redeployed, re-skilled or compensated (see Chapter 4). Lessons from past transitions (e.g. UK coal mine closures of the 1980s, winding down of the shipbuilding industry in Japan) can be drawn upon to inform the development of such policies that will be required at the national, regional and local levels. Empowering local and city governments to plan and finance the transition will be an essential part of creating new jobs, industries, skills and opportunities for all in the low-emission economy (see Chapter 7) (Botta, 2018[39]).

Source: Oluleye, G., N. Shah and A. Hawkes (2018[40]), Emerging Strategies for Decarbonising Energy-Intensive Industries (forthcoming), *Financing Climate Futures Case Studies*, Imperial College London Consultants, London.

References

Ang, G., D. Röttgers and P. Burli (2017), "The empirics of enabling investment and innovation in renewable energy", *OECD Environment Working Papers*, No. 123, OECD Publishing, Paris, *http://dx.doi.org/10.1787/67d221b8-en.* [7]

Baron, R. (2017), *The Role of Public Procurement in Low-carbon Innovation*, OECD Publishing, Paris, *https://www.oecd.org/sd-roundtable/papersandpublications/The%20Role%20of%20Public%20Procurement%20in%20Low-carbon%20Innovation.pdf* (accessed on 23 July 2018). [20]

Botta, E. (2018), "A Review of "Transition Management" Strategies: Lessons for Advancing the Green Low-carbon Transition", *Green Growth and Sustainable Development Forum 2018 Issue Notes*, OECD Publishing, Paris, *http://www.oecd.org/greengrowth/ggsd-2018/.* [39]

Calel, R. and A. Dechezleprêtre (2016), "Environmental Policy and Directed Technological Change: Evidence from the European Carbon Market", *Review of Economics and Statistics*, Vol. 98/1, pp. 173-191, *http://dx.doi.org/10.1162/REST_a_00470.* [8]

Circular Flanders (2017), *Together towards a circular economy: Kick-off Statement*, *http://www.vlaanderen-circulair.be/src/Frontend/Files/userfiles/files/Circular%20Flanders%20Kick-Off%20Statement.pdf.* [17]

Climate-KIC (n.d.), *What is EIT Climate-KIC?*, Climate-KIC Web Portal, *https://www.climate-kic.org/who-we-are/what-is-climate-kic/* (accessed on 26 October 2018). [29]

De La Tour, A., M. Glachant and Y. Ménière (2011), "Innovation and international technology transfer: The case of the Chinese photovoltaic industry", *Energy Policy, Elsevier*, Vol. 39, *http://dx.doi.org/10.1016/j.enpol.2010.10.050.* [37]

Dechezleprêtre, A., R. Martin and S. Bassi (2016), *Climate change policy, innovation and growth*, Grantham Research Institute on Climate Change and the Environment and the Global Green Growth Institute (GGGI), London and Seoul, *http://www.lse.ac.uk/GranthamInstitute/wp-content/uploads/2016/01/Dechezlepretre-et-al-policy-brief-Jan-2016.pdf* (accessed on 18 October 2018). [24]

Energetics Incorporated (2018), *U.S.–China Clean Energy Research Center (CERC)*, *http://www.us-china-cerc.org/overview/* (accessed on 15 October 2018). [30]

European Commission (2018), *Strengthening INternational Cooperation on climatE change REsearch*, *https://cordis.europa.eu/project/rcn/212912_en.html* (accessed on 15 October 2018). [31]

Foray, D., D. Mowery and R. Nelson (2012), "Public R and D and social challenges: What lessons from mission R and D programs?", *Research Policy*, Vol. 41, pp. 1697-1702, *http://dx.doi.org/10.1016/j.respol.2012.07.011.* [10]

Gaddy, B., V. Sivaram and F. O'Sullivan (2016), "Venture Capital and Cleantech: The Wrong Model for Clean Energy Innovation", MIT Energy Initiative, Cambridge, Massachusetts, *https://energy.mit.edu/wp-content/uploads/2016/07/MITEI-WP-2016-06.pdf* (accessed on 02 September 2018). [34]

Glachant, M. and A. Dechezleprêtre (2017), "What role for climate negotiations on technology transfer?", *Climate Policy*, Vol. 17/8, pp. 962-981, *http://dx.doi.org/10.1080/14693062.2016.1222257*. [38]

IEA (2018), *Tracking Clean Energy Progress*, International Energy Agency, Paris, *https://www.iea.org/tcep/*. [4]

IEA (2018), *World Energy Investment 2018*, International Energy Agency, *https://www.iea.org/wei2018/*. [25]

IEA (2017), *Early-stage venture capital for energy innovation: Financing models, trends and implications for policy*, International Energy Agency, Paris, *https://www.iea.org/publications/insights/insightpublications/InsightsSeries2017Early_Stage_Venture_Capital_for_Energy_Innovation.pdf* (accessed on 18 October 2018). [35]

IEA (2017), *Energy Technology Perspectives 2017: Catalysing Energy Technology Transformations*, International Energy Agency, Paris, *https://www.iea.org/etp2017/*. [3]

IEA (n.d.), *IEA Technology Collaboration Programmes: Highlights and Outcomes*, International Energy Agency Web Portal, *https://www.iea.org/tcp/* (accessed on 26 October 2018). [32]

In, S., A. Monk and R. Levitt (2017), *An Integrated Control Tower: Unlocking Long-Term Investment Capital for Clean Energy Innovation*, *https://energy.stanford.edu/sites/default/files/in-levitt-monkpaper_4pub.pdf* (accessed on 03 September 2018). [33]

IPCC (2018), *Global Warming of 1.5 degrees C*, Intergovernmental Panel on Climate Change, Geneva, *http://www.ipcc.ch/report/sr15/*. [1]

Kuittinen, H. and D. Velte (2018), "Energiewende (Germany): Case Study Report", *Mission-oriented R and I policies, in-depth case studies*, European Commission, Brussels, *http://dx.doi.org/10.2777/835267*. [13]

Mazzucato, M. (2017), "Mission-Oriented Innovation Policy: Challenges and Opportunities", *UCL Institute for Innovation and Public Purpose Working Papers*, No. 2017-1, University College London, London, *https://www.ucl.ac.uk/bartlett/public-purpose/publications/2018/jan/mission-oriented-innovation-policy-challenges-and-opportunities* (accessed on 18 October 2018). [11]

Mission Innovation (2018), *About Mission Innovation*, *http://mission-innovation.net/about/* (accessed on 31 August 2018). [26]

O'Donnell, B. and M. Gruenig (2016), *Understanding the Energy Transition in Germany*, Ecologic Institute, Washington, DC, *https://www.ecologic.eu/sites/files/publication/2016/ew_booklet_1.2_0.pdf*. [12]

OECD (2018), *Effective Carbon Rates 2018: Pricing Carbon Emissions Through Taxes and Emissions Trading*, OECD Publishing, Paris, *http://dx.doi.org/10.1787/9789264305304-en*. [9]

OECD (2017), *Green Growth Indicators 2017*, OECD Green Growth Studies, OECD Publishing, Paris, *http://dx.doi.org/10.1787/9789264268586-en*. [2]

OECD (2017), *Public Procurement for Innovation: Good Practices and Strategies*, OECD Public Governance Reviews, OECD Publishing, Paris, *http://dx.doi.org/10.1787/9789264265820-en*. [21]

OECD (2015), *The Innovation Imperative: Contributing to Productivity, Growth and Well-Being*, OECD Publishing, Paris, *http://dx.doi.org/10.1787/9789264239814-en*. [6]

OECD (2014), "China: The Case of Electric Vehicles", in *System Innovation: Case Studies*, OECD Publishing, Paris, *https://www.innovationpolicyplatform.org/system/files/CHINA%20-%20The%20Case%20of%20Electric%20Vehicles-%20IPP_0.pdf*. [14]

OECD (2014), *Research Co-operation between Developed and Developing Countries in the Area of Climate Change Adaptation and Biodiversity*, OECD Publishing, Paris, *http://www.oecd.org/science/Research_Cooperation.pdf*. [27]

OECD (2011), *Demand-side Innovation Policies*, OECD Publishing, Paris, *http://dx.doi.org/10.1787/9789264098886-en*. [22]

OECD (2011), *Invention and Transfer of Environmental Technologies*, OECD Studies on Environmental Innovation, OECD Publishing, Paris, *http://dx.doi.org/10.1787/9789264115620-en*. [36]

OECD (2011), *Towards Green Growth*, OECD Publishing , Paris, *https://doi.org/10.1787/9789264111318-en* (accessed on 23 August 2018). [18]

Oluleye, G., N. Shah and A. Hawkes (2018), "Emerging Strategies for Decarbonising Energy-Intensive Industries (forthcoming)", *Financing Climate Futures Case Studies*, Imperial College London Consultants, London. [40]

Pelkonen, A. (2018), "New Energy Vehicles (China): Case Study Report", *Mission-oriented R and I policies, in-depth case studies*, European Commission, Brussels, *http://dx.doi.org/10.2777/70625.* [15]

Rozenberg, J., A. Vogt-Schilb and S. Hallegatte (2014), *Transition to Clean Capital, Irreversible Investment and Stranded Assets*, World Bank, Washington, DC, *http://hdl.handle.net/10986/18343.* [19]

Société Wallonne du Crédit Social (n.d.), *Société Wallonne du Crédit Social - Web Portal*, *https://www.swcs.be/* (accessed on 18 October 2018). [23]

Tuerk, A. and N. Bird (2018), "Circular Economy Flanders (Belgium)", *Mission-oriented R and I policies, in-depth case studies*, European Commission, Brussels, *http://dx.doi.org/10.2777/8484.* [16]

UN Environment (2018), "Digital Finance and Citizen Action in Financing the Future of Climate-Smart Infrastructure", *Financing Climate Futures Case Studies*, UN Environment. [5]

US Department of Energy (n.d.), *The SunShot Initiative*, United States Department of Energy Web Portal, *https://www.energy.gov/eere/solar/sunshot-initiative* (accessed on 26 October 2018). [28]

Financing Climate Futures
Rethinking Infrastructure

Chapter 4

Ensure fiscal sustainability for a low-emission, resilient future

The climate challenge requires governments to align all channels of public finance with climate and growth objectives, while also taking into account medium-term budgetary cycles and longer-term fiscal sustainability. This chapter describes why public budgets play a central role in creating incentives for shifting finance towards low-emission, resilient investments. It describes barriers facing governments as well as the opportunities to be gained from the transition to a low-emission, resilient economy. Four priority actions are identified: diversify government revenue streams away from fossil fuels, align fiscal policies with climate objectives, align incentives and mandates of all public institutions with climate objectives, and anticipate and address the social consequences of the low-emission transition.

Key messages

The power and influence of public budgets, if channelled towards climate objectives, can provide significant momentum towards building a low-emission, resilient economic future. In order to make meaningful progress on climate, there are four priority policy actions:

- Diversify government revenue streams to prepare for carbon neutrality in the long run, and reduce governments' exposure to incumbents and vested interests in fossil fuel technologies.
- Align fiscal and budgetary incentives with climate objectives to discourage emissions-intensive behaviours or investments by economic actors.
- Leverage public procurement practices and indirect spending through state-owned enterprises, development finance institutions, export credit agencies and public investments to align with climate objectives.
- Ensure an inclusive transition along the way, fostering public support for raising climate ambition.

Why is better public budgeting transformative?

The way governments choose to raise and spend money is decisive in delivering the low-emission, resilient transformation needed. The climate challenge requires governments to align all channels of public finance with climate and growth objectives, while also taking into account medium-term budgetary cycles and longer-term fiscal sustainability.

Through their budgeting processes, policies and fiscal incentives, governments play a central role in directing financial flows and influencing climate-related behaviours of citizens, financiers and businesses. What governments put a price on and what they choose to support financially – for example through carbon pricing and support for renewables – can provide the signals needed to leverage and shift private sector investments towards low-emission and resilient investments.

Reforming the spending policies of public entities can have major impacts on the way in which public expenditures influence climate outcomes. For example, ensuring that the mandates of state-owned enterprises (SOEs), development co-operation agencies, export credit agencies and public investment funds are compatible with climate goals can be a powerful and transformative action. Similarly, the experience of "greening" public procurement processes can be effective in driving innovation and the uptake of new technologies.

Without coherent action, governments – particularly those reliant on fossil fuels as a significant source of revenue – are at risk of not being fiscally sustainable over the long run as fossil fuels are phased out. This not only affects central government revenues, but also the broader economy where businesses, regions and individuals rely on emissions-intensive industries. Countries must be aware of the shifting revenue base that will accompany the low-emission economy. Government revenues will need to adapt to decarbonisation, implying a structural shift away from reliance on revenues from fossil fuel extraction, production and consumption over the long term.

The economic transition will also result in an increased risk of stranded assets and workers who may require government support to minimise the social impacts of the transition. Acting now allows governments to plan and reshape their economies towards a low-emission, resilient future. It allows regions to lead the way in innovative low-emission industries, while building up the competencies and skills of workers to enable them to be employed in a different economic paradigm.

What is the state of play?

Carbon pricing – recognised as an essential element of the climate public budgeting toolkit – is increasing. The number of carbon pricing initiatives has more than tripled in the last 10 years as more governments at the national and subnational level continue to plan and implement carbon pricing initiatives. To date, 45 national and 25 subnational jurisdictions have implemented, or have scheduled for implementation, carbon pricing initiatives (World Bank and Ecofys, 2018[1]). This represents 20% of global greenhouse gas (GHG) emissions, up from 15% in 2017. Despite progress, this is not sufficient to meet the goals of the Paris Agreement. Currently, 88% of energy emissions are priced below EUR 30 per tonne of CO_2, which is a low-end estimate of the damage that emissions cause (OECD, 2018[2]).

On the spending side, while momentum is growing to divest from fossil fuels, global financial support for fossil fuels remains high. Of 76 economies that collectively emit 94% of global CO_2 emissions, aggregate estimates of the annual production and consumption support to fossil fuels ranged from USD 373 billion to USD 617 billion over the period 2010-15 (OECD, 2018[3]).

What are the barriers and opportunities for change?

Political economy and public acceptability concerns are the main barriers to moving from an incremental approach to greening public budgets to a more transformative approach. Decades of fossil fuel development have led to government budgets becoming "entangled" in carbon emissions. Carbon entanglement refers to the state in which fiscal revenues from fossil fuels (for example, from collecting royalties on the extraction of oil, natural gas and coal) form a key part of governments' taxation revenue base. This carbon entanglement is an important political obstacle for governments to engage in the radical transformation needed to transition to a low-emission, resilient future. The share of government revenues coming from fossil fuels averages nearly 8% globally. The situation is very different from country to country: for fossil fuel exporters, this figure can represent over 75% of revenues (see Table 4.1).

As governments undertake the transition away from a fossil fuel based economy, they will inevitably face resistance from a range of stakeholders. They will need to pay greater attention to understanding and addressing the social consequences of the structural shift needed of their economies. Considering the distributional impact of climate policies on poor and vulnerable populations will be key for governments in meeting their social objectives and in reducing any undesirable and unintended distributional impacts of such policies. Certain industries will thrive, while others that are dependent on fossil fuels and are not willing or able to adapt to the new low-emission economy may not fare as well. This means that specific regions, workers, industries and investors may be particularly affected. The use of public resources to address these issues is closely linked to fiscal sustainability through the need to ensure that adequate resources are available, well-targeted and focused on the broad suite of transition measures required (for example, education and reskilling of affected workers).

Table 4.1. **Estimated rents from the extraction of oil, natural gas and coal resources**

	Billions USD			% GDP			% Total government revenues		
Period average	2001-05	2006-10	2011-16	2001-05	2006-10	2011-16	2001-05	2006-10	2011-16
G20 (excl. EU)	**483**	**1015**	**1032**	**1.6**	**2.3**	**1.8**	**4.8**	**7.1**	**5.6**
Argentina	6	12	11	3.6	3.6	2.0	16.4	13.3	6.1
Australia	8	25	24	1.6	2.7	1.7	4.6	7.9	4.9
Brazil	11	29	37	1.8	1.8	1.6	5.1	5.0	4.9
Canada	35	46	24	3.8	3.2	1.4	9.4	8.1	3.6
People's Republic of China	51	180	184	2.9	4.1	1.9	18.2	18.3	6.8
France	0	0	0	<1	<1	<1	<1	<1	<1
Germany	2	5	3	<1	<1	<1	<1	<1	<1
India	13	37	41	2.2	2.9	2.1	11.9	14.8	10.3
Indonesia	11	27	30	5.0	5.3	3.3	27.1	31.8	22.6
Italy	1	2	3	<1	<1	<1	<1	<1	<1
Japan	0	0	0	<1	<1	<1	<1	<1	<1
Korea	0	0	0	<1	<1	<1	<1	<1	<1
Mexico	27	50	47	3.5	4.9	3.9	17.6	21.1	16.7
Russian Federation	82	195	230	16.9	14.5	12.2	44.8	38.6	33.8
Saudi Arabia	91	205	276	38.7	45.2	39.3	>90	>90	>90
South Africa	5	12	9	2.8	4.0	2.5	11.5	14.5	8.8
Turkey	1	2	1	<1	<1	<1	<1	<1	<1
United Kingdom	17	26	19	<1	1.0	<1	2.3	2.6	1.9
United States	119	162	94	1.0	1.1	<1	3.3	3.8	1.8
Rest of World	**304**	**751**	**857**	**3.8**	**5.4**	**4.9**	**3.2**	**15.8**	**15.8**
OPEC (excl. Saudi Arabia)	**178**	**457**	**531**	**26.4**	**26.9**	**25.1**	**30.4**	**78.0**	**84.5**
World	**787**	**1766**	**1889**	**2.0**	**3.0**	**2.5**	**4.0**	**9.0**	**7.7**

Notes: OECD calculations based on World Bank data on oil, natural gas and coal rents and revenue, excluding grants (% GDP). World Bank's oil, natural gas and coal rents have been estimated based on sources and methods described in Lang, G.-M., Q. Wodon and K. Carey (2018[4]), *The Changing Wealth of Nations 2018: Building a Sustainable Future*, World Bank, Washington, DC, *https://openknowledge.worldbank.org/handle/10986/29001*.

Source: World Bank (2018[5]), *World Development Indicators* (database), *https://datacatalog.worldbank.org/dataset/world-development-indicators*.

StatLink https://doi.org/10.1787/888933856378

4.1. Diversify government revenue streams away from fossil fuels

Long-term fiscal sustainability is a central consideration for all governments, but is especially important for those with revenues and economies highly dependent on fossil fuels. The carbon entanglement of government budgets is a major barrier to more ambitious climate action as governments may appear to be acting against their own interest in the short term by moving away from fossil fuels. Carbon entanglement presents a significant risk for countries' medium- to long- term fiscal sustainability as they transition to low-emission economies. Given that declining production and consumption of fossil fuels is a key element of projected decarbonisation pathways to meet the Paris Agreement goals, the prospect of declining tax revenues from fossil fuels raises serious and growing concerns about the future tax base and tax mix.

A successful and decisive transition away from carbon entanglement hinges on effective and strategic planning and is best if done from a position of relative economic strength when international energy prices are high. It will require diversification away from fossil fuels by committing to alternate energy sources and rethinking economic features such as workforce skills, education and training institutions, and infrastructure.

Box 4.1. **Momentum is growing to divest from fossil fuels**

An increasing number of public and private actors have committed to remove investment capital from fossil fuel companies. Some of these pledges have focused exclusively on coal or the most emissions-intensive upstream activities – such as exploitation of oil sands – or the most potentially disruptive to fragile ecosystems – such as greenfield developments in the Arctic. Others have opted to divest from companies with large stakes in the oil, gas or coal industries in general.

National funds

- Dáil Éirann, the lower house of Ireland's parliament, approved a bill mandating the divestment of all fossil fuel company assets managed by the Ireland Strategic Investment Fund by 2023 (Oireachtas, 2016[9]). If parliament's upper house approves the bill, Ireland will need to divest EUR 318 million of the fund's total EUR 8 billion (Carrington, 2018[10]). Ireland's motivations were explicitly climate-related.
- In 2017, Norway's central bank recommended that the Government Pension Fund Global, the world's largest sovereign wealth fund managing over USD 1 trillion, divest from oil and gas stocks (Olsen and Slyngstad, 2017[11]). Unlike the case of Ireland, risk minimisation was the motivation behind Norway's decision.

Cities

- Over 100 municipalities of varying sizes across the globe have also committed to divest including cities and towns in Australia, Denmark, France, Germany, Liberia, the Netherlands, New Zealand, Norway, South Africa, Sweden, the United Kingdom and the United States (Go Fossil Free[12]). Some have committed to full divestment from all fossil fuel company assets, while others aim to divest partially.
- New York City has set an objective to divest USD 5 billion of fossil fuel company assets from its USD 189 billion pension funds within the next five years (Milman, 2018[13]). Other major cities that have committed to divestment include Auckland, Berlin, Bristol, Cape Town, Copenhagen, Melbourne, Paris, San Francisco, Stockholm and Sydney – as well as Oslo's pension fund (Go Fossil Free[12]).

Broadening the tax base, for example by diversifying economic activity, will also be essential to move away from an emissions-intensive economy. As the fossil-fuel tax base erodes, governments will need to compensate for such loss by identifying new streams of revenue, such as the taxation of environmental externalities. In the area of carbon tax, there is significant space for broadening the tax base and increasing rates and, in the short to medium term, this may help to bridge the gap in revenues. However, this will not be sufficient in the long term as emissions decrease, and with it, the tax base. New business models and diversifying economic activity are therefore crucial for expanding the government revenue base to ensure fiscal and economic sustainability.

There are some examples of this in practice:

- Norway manages its oil wealth through a sovereign wealth fund, which has helped citizens achieve high living standards and reduced the country's exposure to fluctuations in the oil price, while also diversifying its economy away from fossil fuel dependence.
- Scotland is aiming for a shift towards an electricity system entirely dependent on renewable energy by 2020. Since 2006, it has seen a four-fold increase in the proportion of electricity

coming from renewables (Government of Scotland, 2018[6]). The transition has had a positive impact regionally, as it included explicit targets for locally-owned power generation plants.

- The state of California, despite being the third-largest producer of oil and gas in the United States, has joined Hawaii in legislating that all electricity be carbon neutral by 2045 (California Energy Commission[7]).
- The United Arab Emirates, the fifth-largest OPEC producer, has committed to diversifying its economy away from oil and natural gas, and sourcing a greater proportion of its electricity from renewables (Government of the UAE[8]).

The twin issues of carbon entanglement and long-term fiscal sustainability are only just beginning to be discussed in government finance ministries (see Box 4.1), yet they are central to the success of the transition to low-emission, resilient economies. There is considerable scope for deepening the debate on this issue and boosting the evidence base to inform future government actions.

4.2. Align fiscal policies with climate objectives

Aligning fiscal policies with climate objectives has long been seen as a core element of the transition to a low-emission, resilient economy (OECD, 2015[14]). Revenue-raising mechanisms, such as carbon pricing, have direct links to climate objectives by shifting behaviours and investments away from emissions-intensive behaviour, and towards innovation in low-emission technologies. Some budgetary support measures, such as fossil fuel subsidies, have the opposite effect by encouraging the production and consumption of fossil fuels and related infrastructure. However, governments should look beyond these core climate policies to ensure the entirety of their fiscal framework are working in unison to achieve a low-emission, resilient future.

Strengthen carbon pricing

Carbon pricing has proven to be a cost-effective climate policy tool if appropriately implemented, and can also offer governments an important revenue-raising opportunity. While the number of carbon pricing initiatives is growing worldwide (World Bank and Ecofys, 2018[1]), there is significant room for improvement (see Figure 4.1).

Exemptions from carbon pricing undermine abatement efforts and increase the overall cost of achieving climate objectives. Looking at the effective carbon price from energy reveals that close to half of CO_2 emissions are not priced at all (OECD, 2018[2]). In most sectors other than road transport (which accounts for 16% of total emissions), a greater proportion of carbon emissions could be priced at a sufficiently high level to induce abatement. The High-Level Commission on Carbon Prices recommends USD 40-80 per tonne CO_2 by 2020 as a range compatible with meeting Paris Agreement goals (2017[15]). Where applicable, countries could increasingly seek to co-ordinate cross-jurisdictional pricing schemes in order to decrease the risk of carbon leakage[1] (Lanzi et al., 2013[16]).

Carbon pricing offers governments an important revenue-raising opportunity. The World Bank Group estimates that governments raised approximately USD 33 billion in direct carbon pricing revenues in 2017, an increase of USD 11 billion from 2016 (World Bank and Ecofys, 2018[1]). Governments have many options at their disposal for using the revenues raised from carbon pricing (see Table 4.2). As with any policy, each of these options requires careful consideration of their respective opportunities and trade-offs depending on the specific circumstances of their jurisdiction. Communicating the use of carbon-pricing revenues, so that citizens can observe the benefits, may assist in reducing resistance to carbon pricing initiatives.

Figure 4.1. **Few countries price a significant share of their energy emissions above EUR 30 per tonne of CO_2 (estimate for 2018)**

Source: OECD (2018[2]), *Effective Carbon Rates 2018: Pricing Carbon Emissions through Taxes and Emissions Trading.*

Table 4.2. **Examples of carbon pricing revenue uses**

	Example
Reduce other taxes	Since introduction of the tax in 2008, British Columbia's uses of carbon tax proceeds include business tax cuts and tax credits, personal income tax cuts (targeted at lower income categories), low-income tax credits and reductions in property taxes
Directing revenues to households	In California, state law stipulates that at least 25% of auction revenues from the state's cap-and-trade programme go to projects that benefit disadvantaged communities – such as the Affordable Housing and Sustainable Communities Program
Providing transitional support to industry	The United Kingdom's national Climate Change Levy addressed the concern of businesses about how they might adjust to potentially higher energy costs
Reducing public debt and/or deficit	The 2010 introduction of the Irish tax on carbon pollution raised much-needed revenue and may have avoided the necessity for even harsher fiscal tightening measures during the economic downturn
Using revenues for general spending	In the EU Emissions Trade System, 9 out of 28 member states (including for example Denmark, Finland, Ireland, Poland, Sweden and the United Kingdom) have opted to direct their auction revenues to their respective national treasuries
Providing funding for climate investments	In Alberta, Canada facilities can directly contribute to the province's Climate Change and Emissions Management Fund as one of the four compliance options under the Specified Gas Emitters Regulation. The fixed fee of CAD 15 per tonne of CO_2 is then used in this dedicated fund to achieve further emissions reductions in Alberta and help the province to adapt to climate change through green technology and innovative solutions.

Source: Adapted from CPLC (2016[17]), *What Are the Options for Using Carbon-pricing Revenues?*, Carbon Pricing Leadership Coalition.

Remove fossil fuel support

A number of budgetary support measures, such as fossil fuel subsidies, still favour emissions-intensive behaviours and practices. Removing inefficient fossil fuel subsidies offers the dual benefit of addressing environmental objectives through the reduction of emissions, while also reducing tax expenditures and simplifying the tax code. Multilateral fora including the G7, the G20 and Asia-Pacific Economic Cooperation (APEC) have all called to reduce inefficient fossil fuel subsidies. Progress is being made; there has been a sustained downward trend in fossil fuel subsidies, partly as a result of falling oil prices as well as reforms by countries such as Mexico and Indonesia. Further progress is expected from the countries that have identified opportunities to remove inefficient subsidies through

APEC or G20 fossil fuel subsidy peer reviews. Fourteen countries have already undergone a review, and Argentina and Canada have committed to undergoing one (IISD, 2018[18]).

Some countries have begun to phase out fossil fuel support measures, but such reforms must be scaled up, mainstreamed, and become part of a more holistic approach to aligning fiscal policies with low-emission outcomes. Finance ministries should carefully review their tax systems, and ensure that taxes and budgetary expenditures are in line with sectoral decarbonisation objectives. A central component of this is to craft fiscal policies that encourage, rather than counteract, the behaviours, investments and practices needed for the radical transformation to move towards a low-emission economy.

Many fossil fuel support measures were introduced prior to 2000 (OECD, 2018[3]). Countries would benefit from critically reviewing their relevance and effectiveness in meeting their policy objectives, particularly in light of climate change, increasing recognition of climate risks, more competitive prices of renewable technologies, and a shift in citizens' priorities. Further work could also be done to create a better understanding of definitions and data on subsidies. Countries require an accurate understanding of the primary impacts on budgets and consumers, in order to effectively reform fossil fuel subsidies. The fossil fuel subsidy peer-review process initiated through APEC and the G20 provides a measure of transparency and an important opportunity for peer learning in identifying and proposing options for the removal of harmful subsidies.

Bring public budgets in line with climate objectives

Beyond direct actions focused on carbon emissions, governments should focus on ensuring that the entirety of their budgetary process is aligned with climate objectives. This can have powerful transformative impacts on the behaviours of consumers and producers, sending political signals on the direction of change, influencing individual and company consumption and production patterns, and leveraging private sector resources for the low-emission transition. The power of this area is yet to be fully realised by governments and there is considerable scope for scaling up activities on public budget alignment.

For example, many countries' fiscal policies provide favourable tax treatment for the use of company cars and commuting expenses, which indirectly results in more cars and more intensive car use. Certain property taxes favour urban expansion and therefore increase commuting distances (see Chapter 7). Corporate tax provisions may also encourage or discourage decarbonisation, for example due to the way corporate taxation allows deductions for different types of capital costs (Dressler, Hanappi and van Dender, 2018[19]). Initiatives such as the Paris Collaborative on Green Budgeting (see Box 4.2) and the Green Fiscal Policy Network aim to align government budgets with environmental and climate goals through fiscal policy reform.

Calculating the full costs of emissions using cost-benefit analysis (CBA) could shift finance towards low-emission, resilient projects. CBA can capture individual projects' climate impact using the social cost of carbon, which measures the present value of the damage resulting from an additional tonne of carbon emissions – or emissions of any other greenhouse gas. For example, particulate matter, sulphur dioxide, nitrous oxides and carbon monoxide can be included in CBAs of transport and energy projects. Environmental CBAs can also capture positive and negative well-being impacts, and can help provide a more holistic picture to decision makers by capturing the co-benefits of low-emission, resilient infrastructure, such as improved air quality, improved access to transport, less traffic congestion and better health (OECD, 2018[20]).

Box 4.2. **The Paris Collaborative on Green Budgeting**

The Paris Collaborative on Green Budgeting was launched by the OECD as part of the 12 announcements presented by French President Emanuel Macron at the 2017 One Planet Summit in Paris. It aims to support governments to assess and drive improvements in the alignment of national expenditure and revenue processes with climate and other environmental goals and to mainstream an environmentally aware approach across all policy domains.

Environmental-responsive or "green" budgeting means using the tools of budgetary policy making to help achieve climate and environmental goals. This includes evaluating environmental and climate impacts of budgetary and fiscal policies and assessing their coherence towards the delivery of national and international commitments, such as the Paris Agreement, the Aichi Targets or the environmentally related Sustainable Development Goals.

Building on international work streams, the Collaborative is an open research platform that brings together environmental, tax, budget and fiscal affairs experts to support peer learning and the exchange of good practices; advance the required analytical and methodological groundwork; and offer targeted assistance for developing a Green Budget Strategy. This includes: proposing, developing and testing pragmatic and transparent tools, such as a Green Budget Statement, to provide an overview of how the annual budget supports achieving environmental goals; guidelines for environmental cost-benefit assessments to support green budgeting; and country scans to investigate the tax revenue effects of environmentally oriented tax policy.

Further information: *www.oecd.org/environment/green-budgeting/*

4.3. Align incentives and mandates of all public institutions with climate objectives

In addition to budgetary processes, governments have significant influence over broader sectors of the economy through public procurement decisions, SOEs, development co-operation, and export credits.[2] By aligning the core mandates and decision-making processes of public institutions with climate objectives, governments can further align their financial flows with a low-emission, resilient future. Sovereign wealth funds and public pension schemes, which typically have significant investments, can build climate objectives into their investment strategies.

Make public procurement a force for change

The significant level of public purchase of goods and services – amounting to 12% of GDP on average among OECD countries (OECD, 2017[21]) – can play a major role in driving low-emission, resilient infrastructure investments. Traditionally, procurement decisions are based on the lowest-cost bidder. Considering life-cycle costing, including life-cycle carbon emissions and other externalities, could help shift procurement decisions towards low-emission options. Building resilience criteria into infrastructure investments is another important way that governments can avoid climate risks (Vallejo and Mullan, 2017[22]).

Adopting new methodologies that take into account externalities could allow for objective evaluation criteria alongside cost (such as carbon emissions). The Netherlands have extensively used the Most Economically Advantageous Tender (MEAT) methodology, which monetises CO_2 performance and the environmental impact of materials (OECD, 2017[23]). Procurement officials and staff need to be sufficiently resourced and trained in order to make public procurement decisions in the interest of a cohesive low-emission transition.

Reorient state-owned enterprises towards low-emission, resilient investments

In many countries, SOEs occupy a central role in the electricity generation sector, accounting for 61% of total global electricity capacity installed in 2016 and approximately 52% of capacity planned or under construction (Prag, Röttgers and Scherrer, 2018[24]). They serve different purposes, such as controlling strategically-sensitive energy supply chains, generating state revenues and securing jobs. As a result of their important presence in these sectors, SOEs are also more exposed to climate change and transition risks. Governments in countries with a high share of SOEs and coal will therefore bear the largest cost associated with the transition if they do not take concrete steps to pivot away from fossil fuels (see Figure 4.2).

Figure 4.2. **Some countries are particularly at risk of stranding coal power plants**

a) Exposure to stranded assets in G20 countries: average age of coal fleet and share of coal in total installed capacity

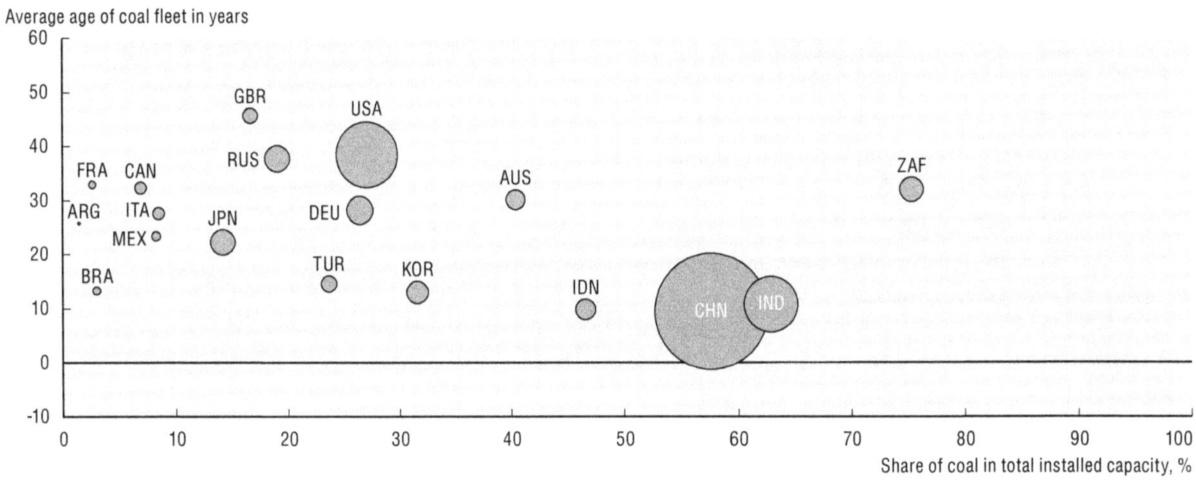

StatLink https://doi.org/10.1787/888933856397

b) Share of SoE ownership and the importance of coal in total installed capacity in G20 countries

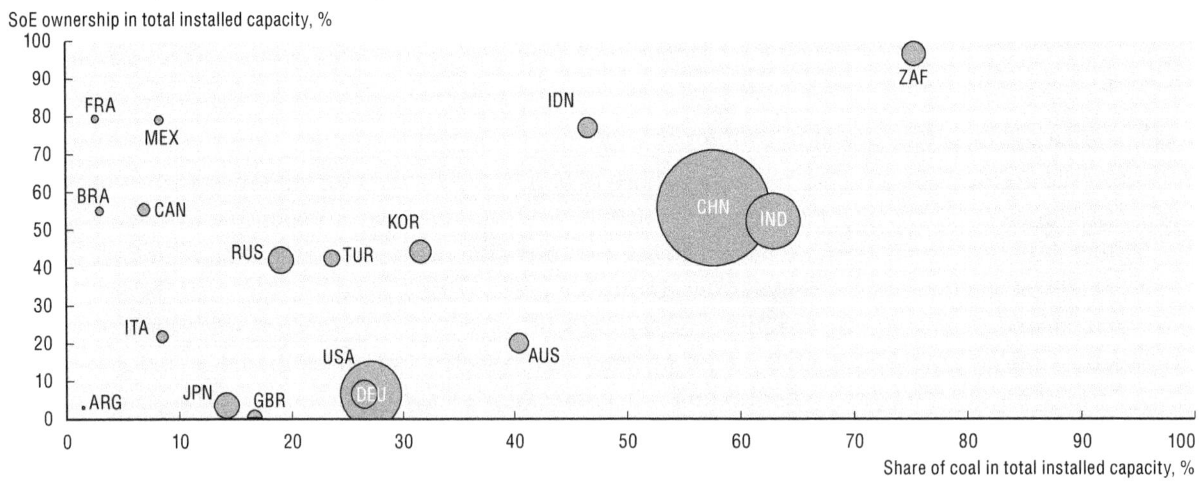

Note: The size of the bubble represents the size of the coal generation capacity stock. The SOE ownership is an estimate based on available SOE ownership data for electricity companies.

Source: Mirabile, M. and J. Calder (2018[25]), "Clean Power for a Cool Planet" (forthcoming), *OECD Environment Working Papers*, OECD Publishing, Paris, *https://doi.org/10.1787/19970900*

StatLink https://doi.org/10.1787/888933856416

Encouragingly, between 2000 and 2014, SOEs in OECD and G20 countries increased the share of renewables in their electricity capacity portfolios from 9% to 23%, leading investments in newly installed renewables capacity (Prag, Röttgers and Scherrer, 2018[24]). This demonstrates that jurisdictions with SOEs in the power market can directly influence the energy mix by investing more in renewable power and less in fossil fuel technologies. Norway's national energy company, formerly known as Statoil, has been rebranded as Equinor in a move towards a more sustainable image. They have committed to investing 15-20% of capital spending by 2030 in renewables, up from about 5% in 2017 (Dagenborg and Adomaitis, 2018[26]).

Mainstreaming climate concerns in SOEs' strategies is an opportunity to influence investment decisions towards low-carbon infrastructure. Decarbonisation efforts could be explicitly and transparently included as public policy objectives in mandates of the SOEs. In addition, SOEs may have access to preferential financing as well as explicit and implicit state guarantees, which translate into lower costs of capital and in turn constitute a substantial competitive advantage in the renewable energy sector, which is dominated by high capital costs (Prag, Röttgers and Scherrer, 2018[24]).

Mainstream climate into development co-operation

Development co-operation plays an important role in supporting action on climate and other environmental issues in developing countries (see Chapter 6). While official development assistance (ODA) makes up only a small share of financing for development when compared with foreign direct investment or government budgets, climate-related ODA is still an important source of support for climate action in developing countries. This includes support to governments and civil society for strengthening the enabling environment – policies, programmes and institutions – for climate-related investments; building the capacity of public and private stakeholders; and mobilising resources for climate-compatible infrastructure. While many middle-income countries will lead the implementation of Agenda 2030 and the Paris Agreement with relatively little external assistance, many others, notably the most vulnerable countries, will require assistance and financial support to make meaningful progress.

For development co-operation to support a transformative shift in countries' development pathways, bilateral portfolios overall need to be aligned with climate goals. The volume of climate-related development finance as a share of overall development finance has been increasing year on year, making up 17.5%, on average, in 2014-15 (see Figure 4.3). However, this suggests that the bulk of bilateral portfolios – over 80% – did not explicitly consider climate change, highlighting an urgent need to better mainstream climate and other environmental objectives across development co-operation, particularly in key natural resources and infrastructure sectors.

It is also important that climate-related support goes beyond business as usual to encourage innovative, targeted solutions that can help countries move away from traditional, emissions-intensive development pathways. Such solutions can include approaches to rapidly scale up commercial investments (Shine and Gampillo, 2016[27]). Currently, bilateral development co-operation providers' approaches to mobilising commercial investment are relatively limited. For example, much of the emphasis on blended finance[3] has been on mobilising different forms of finance from development providers, rather than on attracting commercial investors (OECD, 2018[28]). In addition, more focus is needed on what climate-related development support is used for, rather than on its size. The evidence for what effective climate-related ODA and other official finance looks like remains limited.

Figure 4.3. **The share of bilateral climate-related development finance is increasing**

Two-year averages of commitments in USD billion and shares of total bilateral development finance

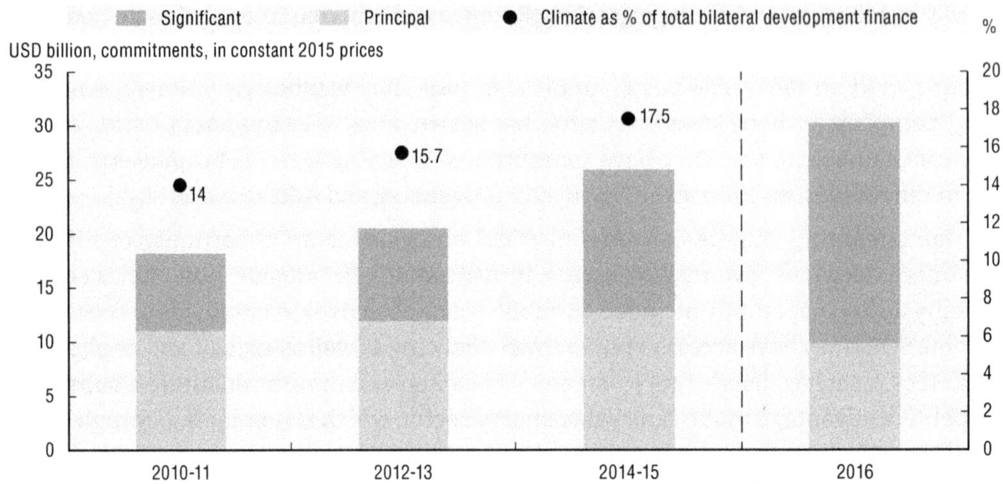

Note: This is based on data reported by OECD DAC members based on the 'Rio Markers' approach, describing policy objectives of the 1992 Rio Conventions on climate change, biodiversity and desertification. Activities marked 'principal' would not have been funded but for that policy objective; activities marked 'significant' have other prime objectives but have been formulated or adjusted to help meet the policy objective.

Source: OECD, *Climate-Related Development Finance 2016*, OECD Publishing, Paris, *https://www.oecd.org/dac/financing-sustainable-development/development-finance-topics/Climate-related-development-finance-in-2016.pdf*

StatLink https://doi.org/10.1787/888933856435

Use export credits or investment promotion agencies to influence sustainable infrastructure

Through export credits, countries can influence the type of infrastructure financed outside their borders. For instance, Gutman et al. (2015[29]) estimate that 20% of external finance for infrastructure projects in sub-Saharan Africa is provided by the People's Republic of China (hereafter 'China') through its institutional bank, EximBank. Historically, the majority of export credits provided by countries that report to the OECD went towards more emissions-intensive sources of power (see Figure 4.4). However, recent years have witnessed an increase in volume of official export credit for renewables. This is being supported by the new rules adopted on export credits for coal-fired electricity generation projects in the run up to COP 21[4] (see Box 4.3).

Box 4.3. **Shifting export credits away from coal-fired electricity generation projects**

To create a level playing field and avoid potential trade distortions, participants to the OECD Arrangement on Officially Supported Export Credits agree to rules on terms and conditions, as well as on the provision of tied aid. Despite the non-binding character of the arrangement, it has been recognised for enhancing transparency and promoting self-regulation in the sector.

In the run-up to COP 21, participants to the arrangement agreed on "The Sector Understanding on Export Credits for Coal-fired Electricity Generation Project", which limits official export credits for the least effective coal-fired plants and encourages exporters and buyers of coal-fired power plants to move away from low-efficiency towards higher-efficiency technologies.

Source: Drysdale, D. (2014[31]), Why the OECD Arrangement Works (even through it is only soft power), *Global Policy*; Levit, J. K. (2004[32]), The Dynamics of International Trade Finance Regulation: The Arrangement on Officially Supported Export Credit, *Harvard International Law Journal*, 45.

Figure 4.4. **Export credits still support fossil fuels for electricity generation**

Countries reporting to the OECD, credit value, USD million

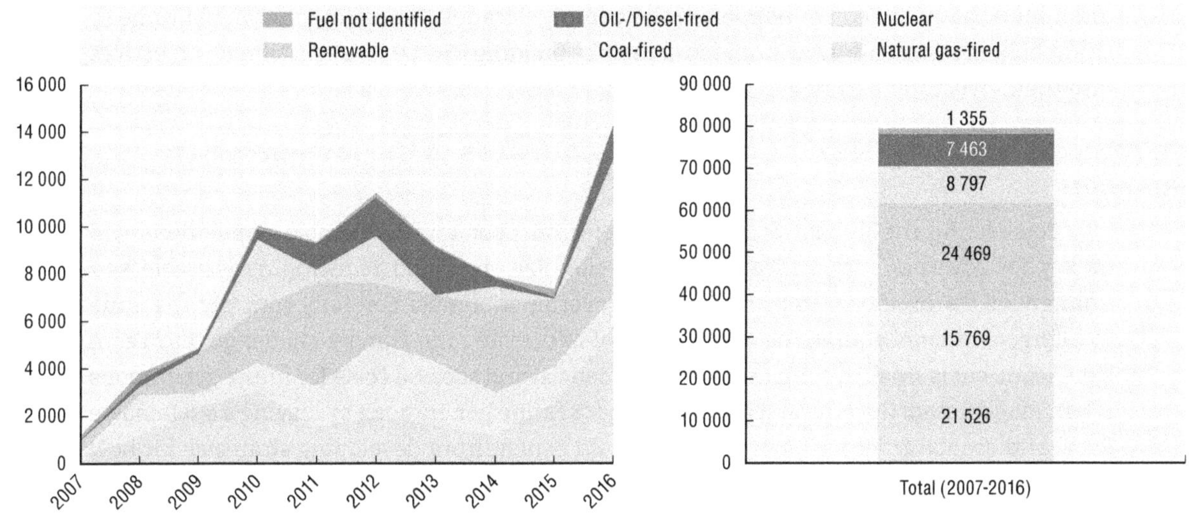

Note: The underlying data set has been drawn from OECD members' individual transaction reporting which covers all official export credits with a repayment term of two years or greater. The data presented are limited to transactions that have been supported according to the terms and conditions of the Arrangement on Officially Supported Export Credits; accordingly, it does not necessarily provide comprehensive figures on the volume of official support provided by members' export credit agencies during the period. Renewables include hydro, solar, wind, geothermal and biomass.

Source: OECD (2017[30]), "Statistics on Arrangement Official Export Credit Support for Electric Power Generation Projects (2007-2016)", *www.oecd.org/tad/xcred/business-activities.htm*.

StatLink https://doi.org/10.1787/888933856454

Public investment can help steer climate action

Governments can be powerful institutional investors, wielding tremendous influence over financial flows through their public investments – sovereign wealth funds (SWFs) and public pension funds in particular. SWFs, for example, are projected to reach over USD 15 trillion by 2020 (One Planet Summit, 2018[33]). Significant fund values and long-term investment horizons make them uniquely positioned to accelerate climate outcomes. Given the significant scale of these funds, building climate objectives into investment decisions is a central way that governments can align financial flows with a low-emission vision of the future.

Countries are stepping up. At the 2017 One Planet Summit, for example, the governments of six large SWFs (France, Kuwait, New Zealand, Norway, Qatar, Saudi Arabia and the United Arab Emirates) joined together to create the One Planet Sovereign Wealth Fund working group. Germany has created a SWF to address the future costs of safely disposing of nuclear waste from energy production; however, the specific details of the investment strategy have yet to be communicated (GeoEconomica, 2017[34]).

Japan's Government Pension Investment Fund (GPIF), the world's largest pension fund valued at USD 1 trillion, has begun to integrate environmental, social and governance (ESG) factors in their investment strategies (GPIF, 2018[35]). Norway's SWF – the largest in the world, valued at over USD 1 trillion and with investments accounting for 1.4% of stocks worldwide – has taken steps to divest coal assets, and has an ambitious proposal to remove oil and gas stocks entirely from the Fund's benchmark (NBIM[36]; Ang and Copeland, 2018[37]). The third-largest public pension fund in the United States, the New York State Common Retirement Fund, announced intentions to divest from fossil fuel investments over the next five years.

Diversifying investments and directing them towards low-emission, resilient infrastructure projects can also help shield public portfolios from a global shift away from fossil fuels that will need to happen in the coming decades. Governments can continue to shift public investments away from fossil fuels by building ESG factors and climate objectives into their investment strategies.

4.4. Anticipate and address the social consequences of the low-emission transition

Considering the impact of climate policies on poor and vulnerable populations will be key for governments in meeting their social objectives and reducing undesirable and unintended distributional impacts. Further, governments must carefully consider the issue of intergenerational equity; the current cost of addressing the climate challenge may seem significant, but is small in comparison to the financial and societal costs for future generations if left unaddressed. Governments should plan for future generations by leaving a sustainable fiscal and economic legacy. Governments would benefit from developing strategies for how to include those worst affected by the transition to a low-emission economy.

Box 4.4. **Lessons from industrial restructuring experiences**

Several regions have demonstrated that a planned transition to a low-emission economy can be successful:

- *New labour policies in response to industrial restructuring in China.* The rapid growth of the Chinese economy has been accompanied by several rounds of large-scale industrial restructuring. In addition, the current overcapacity issues in numerous heavy industries underline an important role for transition management policies in the near future. The policy package initially introduced, which included several instruments such as the establishment of re-employment service centres or financial support measures, have gradually evolved over time.
- *Creating skills for greening existing industries, Flanders (Belgium).* The Flemish chemical and construction sector federation has set up a wide range of activities to address the sustainable skills shortage. These include increased collaboration with universities, "improved branding for the sector", websites to provide information on career perspectives, and collaboration with universities for developing curricula.
- *A "modern transition" strategy: the case of Alberta (Canada).* The Government of Alberta has mandated the phase-out of coal generation by 2029, in line with Alberta's Climate Leadership Plan. On November 2017, it released 35 recommendations to promote a just transition from coal mining, and announced a CAD 40 million transition fund for workers and communities.
- *Overcapacity and labour policies in the fishing industry (Peru).* Substantial overinvestment in vessels, coupled with changes in ocean currents due to climatic events like El Niño, have created significant pressure on the Peruvian fish stock. A reform was introduced in 2017 to improve fisheries management, and supported financial and training support for workers transitioning to other sectors, entrepreneurial training or early retirement. The programme, which was supported by a loan from the World Bank, has been considered successful in decreasing overcapacity and mitigating the associated social impacts.
- *Decline of UK coal mining industry (United Kingdom).* The UK economy once relied overwhelmingly on coal power. Production declined from 130 Mt/year in 1980 to 4 Mt/year in 2015; employment dropped from 237 000 people in 1980 to 1 000 in 2014. A carbon tax in 2016 triggered the most rapid shift in electricity production, from coal to gas. While some new jobs have been created in affected regions, many have been low-paid. Redundancy payments and employment and training advice helped to bridge the gap in employment for affected workers, but regions remain affected.

Source: Enrico Botta (2018[40]), A Review of "Transition Management" Strategies: Lessons for Advancing the Green Low-carbon Transition, *Green Growth and Sustainable Development Forum 2018 Issue Notes*; Fothergill, S. (2017[41]), *Coal Transition in the United Kingdom*, IDDRI and Climate Strategies.

Governments can introduce structural reforms that help firms and workers adjust to market conditions. For example, housing policies could help people move more easily from a low-employment region to a higher-employment region (for example, by improving access to low-cost housing, or decreasing transaction costs). Fiscal policies that favour low-emission innovation and small businesses could result in greater employment opportunities while also benefitting the climate. Revenues from carbon pricing can be used to invest in education, health and clean technology as well as reducing taxes for poorer households (see Section 4.2). Revenues can also be dedicated to improving low-income households' energy affordability (OECD, 2018[38]).

Labour market policies could maintain high levels of employment and a fair distribution of the transitional cost. For example, policies to build active labour markets could help the unemployed find jobs, while skill development systems could smooth workers' reintegration into employment. Demand-side policies can foster a competitive green sector through strong product market competition and moderate employment protection. Income support such as unemployment insurance and work benefits can also ensure a fairer transition for workers (Chateau, Bibas and Lanzi, 2018[39]). Box 4.4 presents some examples from around the world.

Notes

1. Carbon leakage refers to the situation that may occur if, for reasons of costs related to climate policies, businesses were to transfer production to other countries with laxer emission constraints. This could lead to an increase in their total emissions. The risk of carbon leakage may be higher in certain energy-intensive industries.
2. Export credits are government financial support, direct financing, guarantees, insurance or interest rate support provided to foreign buyers to assist in the financing of the purchase of goods from national exporters. Since export credits are commercially motivated and linked to a country's trade strategy, data on export credits are usually not as readily available as data on development finance.
3. Blended finance is the strategic use of development finance to mobilise additional finance for sustainable development in developing countries.
4. The 2015 United Nations Climate Change Conference, COP 21 or CMP 11 was held in Paris, France, from 30 November to 12 December 2015.

References

Ang, G. and H. Copeland (2018), *Integrating Climate Change-related Factors in Institutional Investment*, OECD Publishing, Paris, *https://www.oecd.org/sd-roundtable/papersandpublications/Integrating%20Climate%20Change-related%20Factors%20in%20Institutional%20Investment.pdf* (accessed on 26 July 2018). [37]

Botta, E. (2018), "A Review of "Transition Management" Strategies: Lessons for Advancing the Green Low-carbon Transition", *Green Growth and Sustainable Development Forum 2018 Issue Notes*, OECD Publishing, Paris, *http://www.oecd.org/greengrowth/ggsd-2018/*. [40]

California Energy Commission (n.d.), *California Renewable Energy Overview and Programs*, California Energy Commission, *https://www.energy.ca.gov/renewables/* (accessed on 17 October 2018). [7]

Carrington, D. (2018), "Ireland becomes world's first country to divest from fossil fuels", *The Guardian*, *https://www.theguardian.com/environment/2018/jul/12/ireland-becomes-worlds-first-country-to-divest-from-fossil-fuels* (accessed on 20 July 2018). [10]

Chateau, J., R. Bibas and E. Lanzi (2018), "Impacts of green growth policies on labour markets and wage income distribution: a general equilibrium application to climate and energy policies", *Environment Working Papers*, OECD Publishing, Paris, *https://doi.org/10.1787/19970900* (accessed on 27 September 2018). [39]

CPLC (2017), *Report of the High-Level Commission on Carbon Prices*, *http://www.carbonpricingleadership.org.* (accessed on 06 July 2018). [15]

CPLC (2016), "What are the options for using carbon pricing revenues?", Carbon Pricing Leadership Coalition, *http://pubdocs.worldbank.org/en/668851474296920877/CPLC-Use-of-Revenues-Executive-Brief-09-2016.pdf* (accessed on 19 July 2018). [17]

Dagenborg, J. and N. Adomaitis (2018), "Statoil to rebrand as Equinor in green energy push", *Reuters*, *https://www.reuters.com/article/us-statoil-name-equinor/statoil-to-rebrand-as-equinor-in-green-energy-push-idUSKCN1GR0K2* (accessed on 19 October 2018). [26]

Dressler, L., T. Hanappi and K. van Dender (2018), "Unintended technology-bias in corporate income taxation: The case of electricity generation in the low-carbon transition", *OECD Taxation Working Papers*, No. 37, OECD Publishing, Paris, *http://dx.doi.org/10.1787/9f4a34ff-en.* [19]

Drysdale, D. (2014), *Why the OECD Arrangement Works (even though it is only soft law)*, *https://www.globalpolicyjournal.com/blog/19/12/2014/why-oecd-arrangement-works-even-though-it-only-soft-law* (accessed on 19 October 2018). [31]

Fothergill, S. (2017), *Coal Transition in the United Kingdom*, IDDRI and Climate Strategies, *https://coaltransitions.files.wordpress.com/2016/09/coal_uk_v04.pdf* (accessed on 26 October 2018). [41]

GeoEconomica (2017), *From Nuclear Waste, a New SWF Rises*, GeoEconomica, Geneva, *http://sovereign-investors.com/admin/files/1503830682.pdf* (accessed on 26 October 2018). [34]

Go Fossil Free (n.d.), *Fossil Free: Divestment – Commitments*, *https://gofossilfree.org/divestment/commitments/* (accessed on 20 July 2018). [12]

Government of Scotland (2018), *Increase renewable electricity production*, Scottish Government Web Portal, *https://www.gov.scot/About/Performance/scotPerforms/indicator/renewable.* [6]

Government of the UAE (n.d.), *Energy*, Official Portal of the UAE Government, *https://government.ae/en/information-and-services/environment-and-energy/water-and-energy/energy-* (accessed on 17 October 2018). [8]

GPIF (2018), ESG, Government Pension Investment Fund (GPIF) Web Portal, *https://www.gpif.go.jp/en/investment/esg.html* (accessed on 26 October 2018). [35]

Gutman, J., A. Sy and S. Chattopadhyay (2015), *Financing African Infrastructure: Can the World Deliver?*, Brookings Institution, *https://www.brookings.edu/wp-content/uploads/2016/07/AGIFinancingAfricanInfrastructure_FinalWebv2.pdf* (accessed on 25 July 2018). [29]

IISD (2018), *Argentina and Canada commit to peer reviews of their fossil fuel subsidies under the G20 process*, *http://www.iisd.org/gsi/news-events/argentina-and-canada-commit-peer-reviews-their-fossil-fuel-subsidies-under-g20-process* (accessed on 06 July 2018). [18]

Lange, G., Q. Wodon and K. Carey (2018), *The Changing Wealth of Nations 2018: Building a Sustainable Future*, World Bank, *https://openknowledge.worldbank.org/bitstream/handle/10986/29001/978 1464810466.pdf?sequence=4* (accessed on 05 July 2018). [4]

Lanzi, E. et al. (2013), "Addressing Competitiveness and Carbon Leakage Impacts Arising from Multiple Carbon Markets: A Modelling Assessment", *OECD Environment Working Papers*, No. 58, OECD Publishing, Paris, *http://dx.doi.org/10.1787/5k40ggjj7z8v-en.* [16]

Levit, J. (2004), "The Dynamics of International Trade Finance Regulation: The Arrangement on Officially Supported Export Credit", *Harvard International Law Journal*, Vol. 45, p. 65, *https://ssrn.com/abstract=943588* (accessed on 19 October 2018). [32]

Milman, O. (2018), "New York City plans to divest $5bn from fossil fuels and sue oil companies", *The Guardian*, *https://www.theguardian.com/us-news/2018/jan/10/new-york-city-plans-to-divest-5bn-from-fossil-fuels-and-sue-oil-companies* (accessed on 20 July 2018). [13]

Mirabile, M. and J. Calder (2018), "Clean Power for a Cool Planet (forthcoming)", *OECD Environment Working Papers*, OECD Publishing, Paris, *https://doi.org/10.1787/19970900.* [25]

NBIM (n.d.), *Government Pension Fund Global: The Fund*, Norges Bank Investment Bank (NBIM) Web Portal, *https://www.nbim.no/en/the-fund/* (accessed on 26 October 2018). [36]

OECD (2018), *Cost-Benefit Analysis and the Environment: Further Developments and Policy Use*, OECD Publishing, Paris, *https://doi.org/10.1787/9789264085169-en.* [20]

OECD (2018), *Effective Carbon Rates 2018: Pricing Carbon Emissions Through Taxes and Emissions Trading*, OECD Publishing, Paris, *http://dx.doi.org/10.1787/9789264305304-en.* [2]

OECD (2018), *Inclusive Growth in Seoul, Korea*, OECD Publishing, Paris, *http://dx.doi.org/10.1787/9789264290198-en*. [38]

OECD (2018), *Making Blended Finance Work for the Sustainable Development Goals*, OECD Publishing, Paris, *http://dx.doi.org/10.1787/9789264288768-en*. [28]

OECD (2018), *OECD Companion to the Inventory of Support Measures for Fossil Fuels 2018*, OECD Publishing, Paris, *http://dx.doi.org/10.1787/9789264286061-en*. [3]

OECD (2017), *Investing in Climate, Investing in Growth*, OECD Publishing, Paris, *http://dx.doi.org/10.1787/9789264273528-en*. [23]

OECD (2017), *Public Procurement for Innovation: Good Practices and Strategies*, OECD Publishing, Paris, *https://www.oecd-ilibrary.org/docserver/9789264265820-en.pdf?expires=1532266525&id=id&accname=ocid84004878&checksum=92C48DCCC0CA5761A9C544B663A682AE* (accessed on 22 July 2018). [21]

OECD (2017), *Trends in Arrangement official export credits (2007-2016)*, OECD Web Portal, *http://www.oecd.org/tad/xcred/business-activities.htm* (accessed on 19 October 2018). [30]

OECD (2015), *Aligning Policies for a Low-carbon Economy*, OECD Publishing, Paris, *http://dx.doi.org/10.1787/9789264233294-en*. [14]

Oireachtas (2016), *Fossil Fuel Divestment Bill 2016 – No. 103 of 2016*, *https://www.oireachtas.ie/en/bills/bill/2016/103/* (accessed on 20 July 2018). [9]

Olsen, Ø. and Y. Slyngstad (2017), *Investment strategy for the Government Pension Fund Global*, Norges Bank, *https://www.nbim.no/en/transparency/submissions-to-ministry/2017/investment-strategy-for-the-government-pension-fund-global/* (accessed on 20 July 2018). [11]

One Planet Summit (2018), *12 International Commitments: Stepping up for finance adaptation and resilience to climate change*, One Planet Summit, *https://www.oneplanetsummit.fr/sites/default/files/2018-09/OnePlanetSummit-DP-Engagements-EN.pdf* (accessed on 26 October 2018). [33]

Prag, A., D. Röttgers and I. Scherrer (2018), "State-Owned Enterprises and the Low-Carbon Transition", *OECD Environment Working Papers*, No. 129, OECD Publishing, Paris, *http://dx.doi.org/10.1787/06ff826b-en*. [24]

Shine, T. and G. Gampillo (2016), "The Role of Development Finance in Climate Action Post-2015", *OECD Development Co-operation Working Papers*, No. 31, OECD Publishing, Paris, *https://doi.org/10.1787/18a859bf-en* (accessed on 19 October 2018). [27]

Vallejo, L. and M. Mullan (2017), "Climate-resilient infrastructure: Getting the policies right", *OECD Environment Working Papers*, No. 121, OECD Publishing, Paris, *https://doi.org/10.1787/19970900*. [22]

World Bank (2018), *World Development Indicators (database)*, World Bank Open Data, *https://data.worldbank.org/* (accessed on 26 October 2018). [5]

World Bank and Ecofys (2018), *State and Trends of Carbon Pricing 2018*, World Bank, Washington, DC, *https://openknowledge.worldbank.org/handle/10986/29687*. [1]

Financing Climate Futures
Rethinking Infrastructure

Chapter 5

Reset the financial system in line with long-term climate risks and opportunities

There is an urgent need to mobilise all sources of private finance to scale up and shift infrastructure investment towards low-emission, resilient projects. An array of rules governing the financial system favours the status quo and stands in the way of the necessary reallocation of capital. Decision-making processes are distorted by inadequate climate risk pricing, capabilities and biased incentives in the investment value chain. This chapter reviews the barriers linked to a radical reallocation of capital to low-emission, resilient infrastructure, and proposes three priority actions to scale up and shift investment at scale: integrate climate impacts in investment decisions and strategies, increase transparency and disclosure of climate-related risks and opportunities in financial markets, and bolster the role of financial supervisory authorities to ensure a stable and sustainable financial system.

Key messages

There is an urgent need to mobilise all sources of private finance to scale up and shift infrastructure investment towards low-emission, resilient projects. An array of rules governing the financial system favours the status quo and stands in the way of the necessary reallocation of capital. Decision-making processes are distorted by inadequate climate risk pricing, capabilities and biased incentives in the investment value chain. The following actions will help move sustainable finance from momentum to transformation:

- Encourage the integration of climate impact into investment decisions and strategies to improve climate-risk management strategies.
- Incentivise the disclosure of climate-related risks and opportunities for investors to increase transparency in financial markets.
- Support financial supervisory authority to better assess and manage climate-related risks that could threaten the financial stability of the system in the short and long term.

Why is resetting the financial system transformative?

Infrastructure worldwide has suffered from chronic underinvestment for decades, and current global investments fall short on delivering the services needed for sustainable development. Significant levels of infrastructure investment are needed to maintain and upgrade ageing infrastructure, particularly in high-income countries, as well as to support development and the achievement of the Sustainable Development Goals (SDGs) in developing economies. All sources of finance – public and private – need to be mobilised.

The OECD report *Investing in Climate, Investing in Growth* estimates that USD 6.9 trillion of investment in infrastructure is required annually on average between 2016 and 2030 to meet development and climate needs globally (OECD, 2017[1]). Current spending falls short of this figure; it amounts to only USD 3.3-4.4 trillion dollars annually. Two-thirds of the required infrastructure investments are expected to take place in developing and emerging economies (New Climate Economy, 2016[2]). The additional costs of investing in low-emission, resilient infrastructure are offset by potential fuel savings, and are marginal compared to other infrastructure cost drivers (e.g. corruption levels, efficiency of infrastructure delivery). Developments in low-emission technologies and in the digital economy could actually reduce the demand for infrastructure, and make many low-emission, resilient infrastructure investments cheaper than traditional infrastructure systems.

Making infrastructure compatible with a low-emission, resilient future is therefore not more expensive, but it does require a significant reallocation of capital away from fossil fuel-intensive activities towards infrastructure projects supporting low-emission and resilient energy, transport, land-use and urban systems.

Given the considerable need for long-term infrastructure investment, all sources of finance need to be mobilised. Countries need to improve the efficiency of public investment while mobilising private investment at scale and at pace. Innovative financial instruments, supported by digitalisation, can create new opportunities for diversification of financing sources. They can also help align public and private sector interests in infrastructure provision and management, while optimising the capital structure and reducing the cost of capital for the public sector (OECD, 2017[3]).

What is the state of play?

There is some progress in incentivising private investment in sustainable, low-emission and resilient infrastructure. Carbon pricing policies and targeted incentives to change the relative prices, risks and returns of low-emission, resilient projects have induced visible and dramatic changes in the energy sector. The falling costs of some renewable energy technologies mean that they are now competitive with emissions-intensive alternatives. Many innovative financing mechanisms have been implemented to blend public finance, limit the risk for private actors, and subsidise and incentivise private lending, investments and insurance. For instance, the green bond market increased from just USD 3 billion in 2011 to USD 163 billion in 2018, or to USD 895 billion when including climate-aligned bonds (Climate Bonds Initiative, 2018[4]). International financial institutions are also increasingly using their balance sheets to leverage private capital, alongside measures to de-risk investments by providing capacity building in countries (see Chapter 6).

There is increasing momentum for change in the financial system, with a growing number of initiatives to harness finance to drive the low-emission transition (Maimbo et al., 2017[5]; UNEP Inquiry, 2018[6]). Globally, the number of sustainable finance measures doubled between the end of 2013 and the end of 2017, and international initiatives to promote sustainable finance have quadrupled (UNEP Inquiry, 2018[7]). Notable examples include the Financial Stability Board's Task Force on Climate-related Financial Disclosures (TCFD) and the G20's Sustainable Finance Study Group and Sustainable Insurance Forum (SIF).

However, available indicators show that progress has been patchy and incremental. Overall, infrastructure financing levels remained stable between 2010 and 2016. Institutional investments in low-emission infrastructure are a fraction of the assets under management by institutional investors – amounting to USD 84 trillion in OECD countries. Looking just at large pension funds surveyed by the OECD, direct equity investment in unlisted infrastructure projects of all types accounted for only 1% of their asset allocation in 2015, and green infrastructure accounted for only a fraction of that 1% (OECD, 2017[8]).

The failure to align private investment with a well-below 2°C pathway creates risks for the financial system and the global economy as a whole. In the financial system, investments in emission-intensive projects risk becoming stranded assets in a future with net-zero emissions, or vulnerable to physical damage from climate change and weather-related events. For the global economy, continued investment in assets that are incompatible with well-below 2°C pathways could put the climate objectives of the Paris Agreement out of reach.

What are the opportunities and barriers for change?

Governments have a central role to play in steering financial markets towards better pricing of climate-related risks and opportunities. It is essential that countries improve the overall business and investment environment and develop strong and stable climate policy frameworks to orient their economy away from emissions-intensive activities and level the playing field between low- and high-emission alternatives. However, these changes on their own are not enough (see Chapter 1). It is also essential for investors to have a number of de-risking financial tools and instruments at their disposal, such as public guarantees or blended finance mechanisms proposed by development finance institutions (see Chapter 6). A number of obstacles embedded in current financial systems and regulations are preventing the re-allocation of finance to long-term low-emission infrastructure investments at the pace and scale needed.

Box 5.1. **Breaking silos: Actions to develop sustainable infrastructure as an asset class and address the information gap**

Over the past decade institutional investors, such as pension funds, insurers and sovereign wealth funds, have been looking for new sources of long-term, inflation-protected returns. Increasing numbers of institutional investors are recognising the potential for infrastructure investment to deliver inflation-linked, long-term and stable cash flows. A growing number of investors are also concerned with the potential impact of climate change on their long-term financial performance, and have begun integrating environmental, social and governance considerations into their investment processes. But long-term investors approaching infrastructure face an "information gap", and improved data and information are necessary through the following actions:

1. Mapping finance and risk allocation in infrastructure

- Map investment and financing channels for sustainable infrastructure.
- List instruments and levels of public financial support.
- Create a database of stock and flows of infrastructure projects.

For instance, the OECD-led Research Collaborative on Tracking Private Climate Finance monitors flows of private and public climate finance in an effort to measure the extent to which current financial flows are aligned with the goals of the Paris Agreement.

2. Defining the investment characteristics of infrastructure as an asset class

- Promote a definition of sustainable and quality infrastructure to facilitate data collection on performance and sustainability.
- Promote standardisation and harmonisation of project documentation and disclosure.
- Support initiatives to create infrastructure benchmarks.

The G20 has catalysed efforts to address the information gap. In 2014, for example, the G20 launched the Global Infrastructure Hub (GIH), which aims to provide the private sector with free information about government infrastructure projects. However, to date the GIH has failed to collect data related to the sustainability and the climate impacts of infrastructure projects, contributing to the 'silos' within the G20 process and at the national level. These silos are the result of a lack of communication between communities involved, on the one hand, in infrastructure and finance and, on the other, in sustainability.

3. Mobilising private sector investment in developing countries

- Define measurements and criteria to assess the impact of initiatives that leverage private sector capital in low-emission infrastructure.
- Measure governments' instruments and techniques to attract private sector refinancing in low-emission infrastructure.
- Promote the setting of objectives for using national and multilateral development banks' balance sheets to catalyse investment (see Chapter 6).

Source: OECD (2017[3]), *Breaking Silos: Actions to Develop Infrastructure as an Asset Class and Address the Information Gap*; OECD (2017[1]), *Investing in Climate, Investing in Growth.*

The way climate risks and opportunities are managed, disclosed and mitigated in financial systems remains a key obstacle to developing better risk management strategies. The following are key barriers to a better pricing of climate-related risks and opportunities (UNEP Inquiry, 2015[9]; Maimbo et al., 2017[5]; UN Environment, 2018[10]):

- **Risk pricing**: Risk pricing is currently disconnected from climate-related factors, since the financial system lacks comparable climate-related data and metrics; clear standards and definitions of low-emission, resilient infrastructure; and a financial data or a detailed track record on the financial performance of low-emission, resilient infrastructure projects.
- **Capabilities**: Investors tend to invest in what is familiar to them. Climate-related capabilities need to be enhanced to better handle decision making under uncertainty all along the investment value chain and to break behavioural biases.
- **Biased incentives**: Incentives, institutional norms and regulations that still favour short-termism and the status quo need to be shifted to increase the rate of adoption of low-emission technologies and infrastructure projects.

Now is the time to capitalise on the growing momentum to transform the financial sector, but these barriers must be overcome. It is necessary to break the silos between climate and finance communities to fix incentives, capabilities and climate risk pricing, and embark on local, national and international initiatives that aim to mobilise long-term investment on the one hand, and shift investment towards sustainable infrastructure on the other (see Box 5.1). This collaboration is a necessary condition to create the financial system needed for development in line with climate goals.

5.1. Encourage the integration of climate impacts into investment decisions and strategies

Given the growing threats from climate change, understanding, quantifying and actively managing business exposure to climate-related risks should be an important part of risk management practices in companies' activities and investors' portfolios. There are some encouraging signals from investors that a transition towards more sustainable investments is under way. Many investors have started implementing a variety of measures to adapt their investments to climate risks and benefit from climate-related opportunities (Ang and Copeland, 2018[11]), including:

- **Environmental, social and governance (ESG) integration** with a strong emphasis on climate change. For instance, investors representing over USD 70 trillion have become signatories to the UN Principles of Responsible Investment (UN PRI[12]).
- **Thematic investment**, which refers to investment in thematic funds that are aligned with a low-emission transition, or directly in assets.
- **Best-in-class climate investing**, which only targets investment in the best performing companies within each sector or industry.
- **Exclusionary screening** in the due diligence process, which blacklists sectors or companies based on their carbon footprint. For instance, the Powering Past Coal Alliance brings together over 60 national and regional governments, as well as businesses and organisations, who have collectively agreed to phase out existing coal power and place a moratorium on any new traditional coal power stations without carbon capture and storage (UNFCCC, 2017[13]; Government of Canada, 2018[14]).

- **Divestment**, which is the action of selling off subsidiary business interest or investments because of climate risks (Baron and Fischer, 2015[15]). In 2016, total divestment from fossil fuels represented USD 5 trillion across 76 countries (Arabella Advisors, 2016[16]).
- **Active ownership**, in which equity investors use their ownership stake in a company to influence its decision making.

There are still many uncertainties over the impact of such strategies on aggregate levels of funding. Investment strategies such as best-in-class investing, exclusionary screening or divestment may not necessarily translate into lower investment in emissions-intensive assets, as other financiers may still finance them. Active ownership may contribute more directly to mitigation objectives and have a clearer impact on the real economy (see Box 5.2).

Box 5.2. **Major insurers are divesting from coal and tar sands and engaging with companies to prepare for the low-emission transition**

"A 4°C world is not insurable." – Thomas Buberl, CEO of AXA

Insurance companies are at the forefront of the thinking on how to integrate climate-related risks and opportunities in investment decisions.

At COP 21 in 2015, AXA committed to divesting EUR 500 million from the coal industry. At the One Planet Summit in December 2017, it introduced a policy to stop insuring new coal construction projects or businesses, and pipelines associated with the extraction of tar sands. It increased its divestment objectives to EUR 700 million from oil sands producers and EUR 2.4 billion from the coal industry. It also announced that by 2020 it would seek to increase its green investments from its 2015 goal of EUR 3 billion to EUR 12 billion. In co-operation with the International Finance Corporation (IFC), AXA has launched a USD 500 million facility supporting climate-related infrastructure projects in emerging economies.

The Allianz Group has also made divestment from coal a central part of its climate action. The group withdrew from insuring coal-fired power plants as well as planned and operating coal mines. Its goal is to phase out all investment and insurance coverage of coal companies by 2040. As of November 2018, the group had divested EUR 265 million in equities and EUR 4.8 billion in run-off assets. Like AXA, it currently targets energy and mining companies with 30% or more of their revenues derived from coal, and it will reduce the threshold by 5% increments to reach 0% by 2040.

Limiting insurance coverage, divestment and green investments are important tools at insurers' disposal to take action on climate change, but they can also share their expertise and help companies prepare for a future with lower emissions. AXA, for example, engages directly with companies in key industries such as oil and gas (e.g. BP, Eni, Royal Dutch Shell, Lukoil), utilities (e.g. EDF, GDF Suez, RWE, E. ON), mining (e.g. Rio Tinto, Glencore Xstrata, BHP Billiton) and automotive manufacturing (e.g. BMW, Renault, Toyota, Volkswagen). It encourages them to improve disclosure of climate-related risks and develop strategies to manage the global transition towards a low-emission, resilient future.

Source: AXA (2018[17]), "Active engagement: Initiatives 2017/18", AXA website, 3 April 2018; AXA (2017[18]), Integrated Report 2017; Allianz (2018[19]), "Allianz is driving change toward a low-carbon economy with an ambitious climate change package", Allianz website, 4 May 2018.

Mainstreaming climate considerations in investment decisions and strategies across the entire financial system requires action on different fronts: enhancing market transparency; developing benchmarks and metrics of success; valuing risk in the financial system; mapping investments; and harnessing digital finance.

Enhancing market transparency and improving data

Enhancing greater market transparency and improving data on performance, risks and costs and opportunities of low-emission and resilient investments across available channels is essential for promoting sustainable infrastructure as an asset class and leveraging long-term investment (OECD, 2017[3]). The deployment of blockchain technologies could help enable this transparency, provided that the right regulations are in place (see Box 5.3).

Developing benchmarks and metrics of success

Developing benchmarks and metrics of success could facilitate due diligence of low-emission infrastructure and asset allocation modelling (OECD, 2015[20]) and measure performance to feed into the asset allocation process. Establishing a harmonised definition of sustainable infrastructure could be essential to ensure consistency of data collection and help harmonise project preparation. For example, this could be done through SOURCE, an online platform developed by the multilateral development banks (MDBs) to present sustainable, bankable and investor-ready infrastructure projects and improve project preparation.

In 2017, G7 world leaders endorsed the Ise-Shima principles for promoting quality infrastructure investment, and encouraged all actors in the value chain to align their infrastructure investment and assistance with the principles. Building on these principles, the Inter-American Development Bank (IDB) developed a framework for sustainable infrastructure to attempt to harmonise existing definitions of sustainable infrastructure (see Figure 5.1).

Valuing risk in the financial system

Ensuring that investors take climate-related risks and opportunities into account is a critical step in shifting financial flows. This will require a range of interventions to value risks, including broadening concepts of risk and the time horizons over which they are assessed, embedding climate considerations into incentive structures and the key performance indicators of financial decision makers, and mainstreaming related concepts into professional education programmes. Regulators have a key role to play in this regard (see Section 5.3).

Mapping investors channels

Improving the understanding of how financial policies and regulations affect low-emission, resilient infrastructure investment patterns is key. This includes developing better classification systems for financial measures, effective frameworks to measure impact, and enhanced understanding of the transferability of measures across countries at different stages of development and with different financial systems (UNEP Inquiry, 2018[7]).

Figure 5.1. **The IDB's four dimensions of sustainable infrastructure**

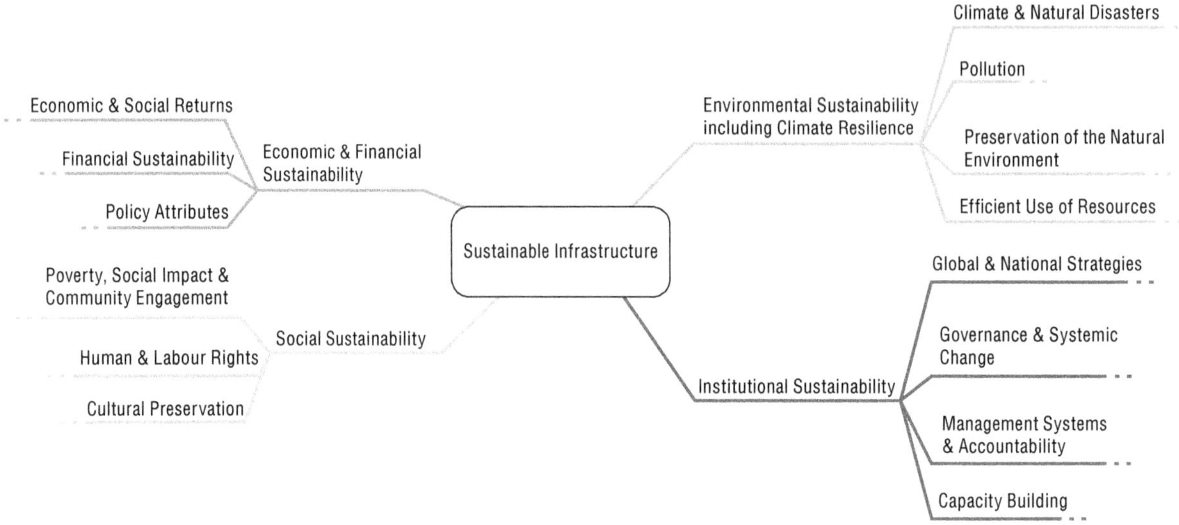

Source: IDB (2018[21]), *What is Sustainable Infrastructure? A Framework to Guide Sustainability Across the Project Cycle.*

Harnessing digital finance

Harnessing the new opportunities created by digital finance could also transform the infrastructure investment value chain, enable citizens to participate more directly in investment and unlock new sources of finance for infrastructure. Chapter 3 has already discussed the example of the M-Akiba retail bond issued by the Government of Kenya, which offers Kenyan citizens the opportunity to invest directly in new and ongoing infrastructure development projects through their mobile phones (see Chapter 3).

Box 5.3. **Blockchain technology could enable more sustainable infrastructure investment**

A number of digital innovations are emerging in the infrastructure space, which offer the potential to transform how physical systems operate by making infrastructure more connected, intelligent and efficient, including blockchain. Blockchain is one of such technologies that can be used for record keeping, automation of processes and transactions, and transferring value through cryptocurrencies or tokens without requiring a central entity to validate transactions.

When thinking about blockchain, carbon neutrality is not the first thing that comes to mind and there are concerns around the technology's CO_2 impacts as vast amounts of energy are required to sustain the network. However, blockchain can also help fight climate change. It can help unlock new sources of financing, serve as a clean energy trading platform, and address key issues along the infrastructure value chain:

- Greater contractual and financial standardisation during the bidding and procurement stages of infrastructure projects can reduce costs and complexity, facilitate comparability of projects, and help financial allocations by investors.
- Enhanced data availability, transparency, privacy and quality can support well-informed investment decisions. Coupled with Artificial Intelligence (AI) technologies for example, blockchain can improve data analytics of infrastructure systems and provide global visibility over climate actions, help track climate financing flows, and encourage greater alignment of these flows.
- Better data on the identification, measurement and management in investment risks can improve risk mitigation.

Box 5.3. **Blockchain technology could enable more sustainable infrastructure investment** *(cont.)*

Some concrete applications of blockchain technologies can help progress towards the goals of the Paris Agreement. For example, as a decentralised financing infrastructure, blockchain-based platforms can enable a wide spectrum of investors to invest directly in low-emission projects. Blockchain can also improve the way emissions trading systems work, by strengthening data transparency and reliability (e.g. on quotas and certificates circulation) and by automating transactions and price discovery. Contract management systems that rely on blockchain can also be applied to keep track of the validity of legally-binding contracts in infrastructure projects, which is particularly appealing with multi-party contract agreements.

However, blockchain's ultimate impact will depend on the ability of governments to develop the right policies to extract its potential benefits and mitigate environmental impacts, while also addressing risks and potential for misuse. Several areas are calling for greater attention:

- **Encouraging collaboration and innovation**: Governments, international organisations, such as the United Nations Framework Convention on Climate Change (UNFCCC), technology providers and academia could form dedicated working groups to support the development of technical standards related to blockchain technologies, building on existing industry alliances.
- **Supporting education**: More research and outreach on blockchain could be supported to develop low-emission related solutions, raise awareness on the technology (e.g. energy consumption, scalability drawbacks), help overcome knowledge gaps, and encourage greater trust in incorporating the technology into current systems.
- **Mitigating environmental impacts**: Governments need to engage with industry to ensure that the protocols and network designs they develop are as energy efficient as possible, and green applications of blockchain technologies (e.g. in energy, transport, trade and agriculture sectors) are playing their role in the low-emission transition.
- **Ensuring supportive regulatory environments**: The regulations that apply to blockchain technologies vary from country to country, and because of the distributed nature of networks, many legal questions are still open. For example, issues related to liability, intellectual property or data privacy are yet to be resolved, and call for careful government attention.

Source: OECD (2018[22]), Blockchain, infrastructure and the low-emission transition (forthcoming), *Financing Climate Futures Case Studies*.

5.2. Encourage the disclosure of climate-related risks and opportunities in financial markets

There is a growing awareness that inadequate disclosure of climate-related risks and opportunities can lead to a mispricing of assets and capital. For instance, investors with some fossil fuel assets might not be able to recover their investment fully due to more stringent climate regulations, but this is not properly accounted for in financial actors' allocation decisions. Three types of climate-related risks could inflict potential losses on investors, and eventually challenge the stability of the financial system (Carney, 2018[23]):

1. Physical risks related to the increased frequency and severity of climate- and weather-related events could damage property and disrupt trade (see Chapter 1). There is growing evidence suggesting that developing countries vulnerable to climate change are experiencing a higher sovereign cost of debt due to climate factors, and that this might increase in the future (Buhr et al., 2018[24]).

2. Liability risks arising if those suffering from climate change losses seek compensation from those they hold responsible. For instance in October 2018 a court in The Hague upheld a historic legal order urging the Dutch government to accelerate carbon emissions cuts (Nelsen, 2015[25]).
3. Transition risks caused by the revaluation of assets in a lower-emission economy. Building more fossil fuel dependent infrastructure will result in stranded assets, defined as assets that are "unable to recover their investment cost as intended, with a loss of value for investors" (Baron and Fischer, 2015[15]). This risk is particularly acute for investors that are closely linked to coal mining or energy production from coal.

Inadequate disclosure could also hide some opportunities to invest in profitable projects created by the low-emission transition. The International Finance Corporation (IFC) estimates that the Paris Agreement could help open up nearly USD 23 trillion in opportunities for low-emission, resilient investments in emerging markets between now and 2030 (IFC, 2016[26]). Such opportunities range from green buildings in East Asia (USD 16 trillion), sustainable transport in Latin America (USD 2.6 trillion), renewables in the Middle East and North Africa, climate-resilient infrastructure in South Asia (USD 2.2 trillion), clean energy in Africa (USD 783 billion) and energy efficiency and transport in Eastern Europe (USD 665 billion) (IFC, 2016[26]).

Measuring and disclosing adequate climate-related information is a first step in making markets more efficient and economies more resilient. Private investors and governments alike can make better decisions with improved transparency and access to information on the climate-related performance and exposure of assets and businesses, as well as financial systems as a whole. In fact, not disclosing climate-related financial information would amount to knowingly excluding key information on risk factors that would lead to mispricing, biased investment decisions and suboptimal investment outcomes.

Many investors and corporations are actively advancing the climate-related disclosure agenda. For instance, at the One Planet Summit in 2017 (see Box 5.4), the Climate Action 100+ coalition, representing 225 investors with USD 26.3 trillion of assets under management, committed to engage with the 100 most polluting corporations, responsible for about two-thirds of worldwide industrial emissions, and to step up their ambition on climate action (Ang and Copeland, 2018[11]). At the same event, financial institutions responsible for managing USD 80 trillion of assets – equivalent to annual global GDP – publicly supported the Task Force on Climate-related Financial Disclosures (TCFD) (see Box 5.5).

Some governments are expanding the disclosure requirements for private and long-term investors. A study by the Cambridge Centre for Sustainable Finance estimates that two thirds of G20 member states have engaged with the TCFD recommendations in some form, mainly through statements of support for the aims and recommendations of the Task Force (CISL, 2018[27]). Australia, Canada, the EU, Italy, Japan, South Africa, Turkey and the United Kingdom have conducted (or are in the process of conducting) consultations with the private sector on sustainable finance generally and on disclosure requirements as an important building block of sustainable finance more specifically. Japan has issued voluntary disclosure guidelines and the EU has put together a firm action plan on how to incorporate the recommendations into existing disclosure frameworks.

Box 5.4. **One Planet Summit's 12 commitments**

In December 2017, leaders from around the world gathered in Paris, France for the first One Planet Summit to speed up the global transition to a low-emission economy. The summit resulted in twelve climate commitments:

Stepping up for finance adaptation and resilience to climate change:

1. Responding to extreme events in island states
2. Protecting land and water against climate change
3. Mobilising researchers and young people to work for the climate
4. Public procurement and access for local governments to green financing

Accelerating the transition towards a decarbonised economy:

5. Zero-emissions target
6. Sectoral shifts towards a decarbonised economy
7. Zero-pollution transport
8. Towards a carbon price compatible with the Paris Agreement

Anchoring climate issues at the centre of the decisions of finance and its actors:

9. Actions of central banks and businesses
10. International mobilisation of development banks
11. Commitment by sovereign funds
12. Mobilising institutional investors

Source: One Planet Summit (2017[28]), "Commitments", One Planet Summit web site, *https://www.oneplanetsummit.fr/en*

In a parallel development to the TCFD, France has required asset owners and investment managers to disclose climate-related financial risks. Under Article 173-VI of the Energy Transition Act, institutional investors must provide information not only on how they integrate ESG factors in their investment and voting decisions, but also on the climate risks they face and how their portfolio's makeup contributes to the transition to a low-emission economy (CISL, 2018[27]). In South Africa, investors must consider how environmental factors can affect long-term performance as per the South African Pension Act (Maimbo et al., 2017[5]).

An important element of the disclosure agenda is the necessity to change the paradigm surrounding disclosure. Instead of disclosing and measuring emissions with static foot-printing techniques, the TCFD encourages the use of scenario analysis to consider dynamically the potential impact of the risks and opportunities of the transition to a low-emission economy on strategy and financial planning.

Reporting practices could move towards the measurement of the emissions embedded in coal, oil and gas reserves and resources. They could include scenario analysis to stress-test investors and companies' portfolios against decarbonisation scenarios and track progress of companies towards science-based targets. Such disclosure would help to better understand the risks for investments that are misaligned with climate goals, differentiated into financial risks and impact risks. Such practices would trigger the behavioural change needed by investors and financiers, and help move away from incremental progress to the radical reallocation needed (TCFD, 2017[29]).

Building climate-related capacity among investors and private firms is an essential factor of success. Low-emission, resilient strategies and science-based targets need to be developed, data on climate-related risks and opportunities of businesses and portfolios need to be collected and reporting on climate-related risks will need to broaden and improve. Regulators and standard-setters could provide guidance to ensure the credibility and comparability of commitments.

Improving climate-related risk assessment and disclosure may not necessarily lead to the desired behavioural change in cases where such risk is still considered acceptable. Such measures should be part of a set of policies that make climate-related risk of material relevance to investors, and a broader disclosure agenda that could encourage more transparency about the financial flows themselves. Improving transparency on financial flows that contribute to the desired transition, as well as on flows that potentially undermine it, could help governments measure progress towards aligning all flows with a low-emission future.

Box 5.5. **What do investors need to disclose about climate?**

The Task Force on Climate-related Financial Disclosure (TCFD) was established by the Financial Stability Board (FSB) in response to a call from G20 Leaders. It has designed a set of recommendations to "shift financial flows towards a low-carbon economy and to avoid stranded assets, reduce or better manage climate-related risks for individual investors, corporates and reduce climate-related risks for the financial system as a whole". It delivered recommendations for voluntary disclosures of material, decision-useful climate-related financial risks for the G20 Summit in Hamburg in 2017.

The recommendations promoted by the TCFD are articulated around the disclosure of four essential elements:

- **Governance:** disclosing the governance of climate-related risks and opportunities;
- **Strategy:** disclosing actual and potential impacts of climate-related risks and opportunities on the organisation's businesses, strategy and financial planning where such information is material;
- **Risk management:** disclosing risk management arrangements for how the organisation identifies, assesses and manages climate-related risks; and
- **Metrics and targets**: disclosing metrics and targets used to assess and manage relevant climate-related risks and opportunities, where such information is material.

The task force also encourages companies to carry out scenario analysis: while some are already affected by risks associated with climate change today, for many the most significant effects of climate change are likely to emerge over the medium to longer term and their timing and magnitude are uncertain. To appropriately incorporate the potential climate effects in their planning processes, companies need to consider how their climate-related risks and opportunities may evolve under different plausible futures.

Source: TCFD (2017$_{[29]}$), *Recommendations of the Task Force on Climate-related Financial Disclosures.*

5.3. Rethink financial supervision in light of climate imperatives

Financial stability is a prerequisite to any type of investment, including investment in low-emission, resilient infrastructure, and the primary role of financial regulators is to ensure the stability of the financial system. There is a growing awareness among regulators and financial supervisors that success in transitioning to a world with manageable levels of climate change is a determinant of financial stability in the long run. The G20 sustainable finance study group stated that "a proper framework for sustainable finance development may also improve the stability and efficiency of the financial markets by adequately addressing risks as well as market failures such as externalities" (G20 Green Finance Study Group, 2016[30]). As a first step, climate considerations need to be integrated into the rules and regulations that support the stability of the financial system.

Progress on this front has already been made. The European Commission's High-Level Expert Group has recommended integrating sustainability into the European Union's regulatory and financial policy framework (see Box 5.6). At the One Planet Summit in December 2017, central banks and supervisors from three continents, including the Bank of England, *Banque de France*, *De Nederlandsche Bank*, *Deutsche Bundesbank* and the Federal Financial Supervisory Authority of Germany *BaFin*, created the network for "greening the financial system", an initiative to help accelerate climate mainstreaming in financial supervision and in the refinancing of secondary markets to promote an orderly development of green finance (One Planet Summit, 2017[27]). The network's ambition is to exchange experiences, share best practices, contribute to the development of environment and climate risk management in the financial sector and mobilise mainstream finance to support the transition towards a sustainable economy, on a voluntary basis.

While recognising that national circumstances matter and that there is no one-size-fits-all approach, governments, financial regulators and climate policy makers can act on a variety of levels (Maimbo et al., 2017[5]):

- Support the growth of low-emission, resilient investment market through the development of standards and policy frameworks that promote the issuance of low-emission, resilient financial products and the emergence of new market platforms. Policy banks and state-controlled financial institutions, including sovereign wealth funds, could be harnessed more effectively (see Chapter 4).
- Continuously monitor the potential unintended consequences of financial regulations and regulatory reforms on the supply of long-term investment financing for climate (Ang, Röttgers and Burli, 2017[31]). This could include preserving the integrity of standards for "low-emission" labels and markets or initiatives such as the emerging global dialogue on capital risk weightings.
- Promote transparency in the financial system, through policies and regulations that support the disclosure of risks and opportunities associated with climate change, disclosure of financial flows, and developing climate-scenario analysis for insurance companies and banks. These scenarios could be a strategic tool for policy making.
- Clarify legal frameworks and mandates for instance on the interpretation of long-term investor obligations and responsibilities in the context of climate change or how climate considerations can be interpreted within the existing mandates of supervisory bodies. For instance, the Central Bank of Brazil has published guidelines for the social and environmental responsibility of financial institutions (Resolution no. 4327 of 2017) (Maimbo et al., 2017[5]; OECD, 2017[32]).

Box 5.6. **European Commission's Action Plan on Financing Sustainable Growth**

In September 2016, the European Commission launched the industry-led High-Level Expert Group (HLEG) on Sustainable Finance to examine how to integrate sustainability considerations into the European Union's financial policy framework.

The HLEG's interim report (June 2017) recommended integrating sustainability into the EU's regulatory and financial policy framework, including through climate disclosure, accounting, fiduciary duties, corporate governance and reporting, and stewardship codes. Its final report stressed that moving towards sustainable finance involves two imperatives: (1) improving the contribution of finance to sustainable and inclusive growth and the mitigation of climate change; and (2) strengthening financial stability by incorporating environmental, social and governance (ESG) factors into investment decision making. The report lays out 30 proposals, including 8 key recommendations.

Building on the recommendations provided in the HLEG's final report, in March 2018 the European Commission launched a broad Action Plan on Financing Sustainable Growth, laying down the roadmap to integrating sustainability in the financial system at the EU level. This involved 10 main actions:

1. Establishing an EU classification system for sustainable activities
2. Creating standards and labels for green financial products
3. Fostering investment in sustainable projects
4. Incorporating sustainability when providing financial advice
5. Developing sustainability benchmarks
6. Better integrating sustainability in ratings and market research
7. Clarifying institutional investors' and asset managers' duties
8. Incorporating sustainability in prudential requirements
9. Strengthening sustainability disclosure and accounting rule-making
10. Fostering sustainable corporate governance and attenuating short-termism in capital markets.

The European Commission announced its first four proposals to support sustainable finance in the European Union in May 2018, and proposed legislation on benchmarks, green definitions, investor duties and retail investing.

Sources: EU High-Level Expert Group on Sustainable Finance (2017[33]); *Financing a Sustainable European Economy: Interim Report*; EU High-Level Expert Group on Sustainable Finance (2018[34]), *Financing a Sustainable European Economy: Final Report*; European Commission (2018[35]), *Action Plan: Financing Sustainable Growth*.

References

Allianz (2018), *Allianz is driving change toward a low-carbon economy with an ambitious climate protection package*, Allianz Web Portal, *https://www.allianz.com/en_GB/press/news/business/insurance/180504-allianz-announces-climate-protection-package.html* (accessed on 19 October 2018). [19]

Ang, G. and H. Copeland (2018), *Integrating Climate Change-related Factors in Institutional Investment*, OECD Publishing, Paris, *https://www.oecd.org/sd-roundtable/papersandpublications/Integrating%20Climate%20Change-related%20Factors%20in%20Institutional%20Investment.pdf* (accessed on 26 July 2018). [11]

Ang, G., D. Röttgers and P. Burli (2017), "The empirics of enabling investment and innovation in renewable energy", *OECD Environment Working Papers*, No. 123, OECD Publishing, Paris, *http://dx.doi.org/10.1787/67d221b8-en*. [31]

Arabella Advisors (2016), *The Global Fossil Fuel Divestment and Clean Energy Investment Movement*, *https://www.arabellaadvisors.com/wp-content/uploads/2016/12/Global_Divestment_Report_2016.pdf* (accessed on 27 July 2018). [16]

AXA (2018), *Active engagement: Initiatives 2017/18*, AXA Web Portal, *https://www.axa-im.com/en/content/-/asset_publisher/alpeXKk1gk2N/content/insight-annual-report-active-engagement/23818* (accessed on 19 October 2018). [17]

AXA (2017), *Integrated Report 2017*, AXA, *https://www-axa-com.cdn.axa-contento-118412.eu/www-axa-com%2F2d414b6f-ac38-44ad-bf1d-0fc4b2a231f2_axa-ra2017-en-pdf-e-accessible_03.pdf* (accessed on 19 October 2018). [18]

Baron, R. and D. Fischer (2015), *Divestment and Stranded Assets in the Low-carbon Transition*, OECD Publishing, Paris, *https://www.oecd.org/sd-roundtable/papersandpublications/Divestment%20and%20Stranded%20Assets%20in%20the%20Low-carbon%20Economy%2032nd%20OECD%20RTSD.pdf* (accessed on 19 October 2018). [15]

Buhr, B. et al. (2018), *Climate Change and the Cost of Capital in Developing Countries*, Imperial College Business School and SOAS University of London, *https://imperialcollegelondon.app.box.com/s/e8x6t16y9bajb85inazbk5mdrqtvxfzd* (accessed on 27 July 2018). [24]

Carney, M. (2018), *A Transition in Thinking and Action*, *https://www.bankofengland.co.uk/-/media/boe/files/speech/2018/a-transition-in-thinking-and-action-speech-by-mark-carney.pdf* (accessed on 14 September 2018). [23]

CISL (2018), *Sailing from different harbours: G20 approaches to implementing the recommendations of the Task Force on Climate-related Financial Disclosures*, University of Cambridge Institute for Sustainability Leadership (CISL), Cambridge, *https://www.cisl.cam.ac.uk/resources/publication-pdfs/cisl-tcfd-report-2018.pdf* (accessed on 25 October 2018). [27]

Climate Bonds Initiative (2018), *Green Bond Highlights 2017*, *https://www.climatebonds.net/files/reports/cbi-green-bonds-highlights-2017.pdf* (accessed on 24 July 2018). [4]

EU High-Level Expert Group on Sustainable Finance (2018), *Financing a Sustainable European Economy: Final Report*, European Commission, *https://ec.europa.eu/info/sites/info/files/180131-sustainable-finance-final-report_en.pdf* (accessed on 05 July 2018). [34]

EU High-Level Expert Group on Sustainable Finance (2017), *Financing a Sustainable European Economy: Interim Report*, European Commission, *https://ec.europa.eu/info/sites/info/files/170713-sustainable-finance-report_en.pdf* (accessed on 13 September 2018). [33]

European Commission (2018), *Action Plan: Financing Sustainable Growth*, *http://eur-lex.europa.eu/legal-content/EN/TXT/?qid=1483696687107&uri=CELEX:52016SC0405.* (accessed on 05 July 2018). [35]

G20 Green Finance Study Group (2016), *G20 Green Finance Synthesis Report*, G20 Green Finance Study Group, *http://www.g20.utoronto.ca/2016/green-finance-synthesis.pdf* (accessed on 12 September 2018). [30]

Government of Canada (2018), *Power Past Coal Alliance Declaration*, *https://www.canada.ca/en/services/environment/weather/climatechange/canada-international-action/coal-phase-out/alliance-declaration.html* (accessed on 20 July 2018). [14]

IDB (2018), *What is Sustainable Infrastructure? A Framework to Guide Sustainability Across the Project Cycle*, Inter-American Development Bank, *https://publications.iadb.org/bitstream/handle/11319/8798/What-is-Sustainable-Infrastructure-A-Framework-to-Guide-Sustainability-Across-%20the-Project-Cycle.pdf?sequence=1&isAllowed=y* (accessed on 24 July 2018). [21]

IFC (2016), *Climate Investment Opportunities in Emerging Markets*, International Finance Corporation, Washington, DC, *https://www.ifc.org/wps/wcm/connect/51183b2d-c82e-443e-bb9b-68d9572dd48d/3503-IFC-Climate_Investment_Opportunity-Report-Dec-FINAL.pdf?MOD=AJPERES* (accessed on 19 October 2018). [26]

Maimbo, S. et al. (2017), "Roadmap for a Sustainable Financial System", No. 121283, World Bank Group and UNEP Inquiry, Washington, DC, *http://documents.worldbank.org/curated/en/903601510548466486/Roadmap-for-a-sustainable-financial-system*. [5]

Nelsen, A. (2015), "Dutch government ordered to cut carbon emissions in landmark ruling", *The Guardian*, *https://www.theguardian.com/environment/2015/jun/24/dutch-government-ordered-cut-carbon-emissions-landmark-ruling* (accessed on 19 October 2018). [25]

OECD (2018), "Blockchain, infrastructure and the low-emission transition (forthcoming)", *Financing Climate Futures Case Studies*, OECD Publishing, Paris. [22]

OECD (2017), *Breaking Silos: Actions to Develop Infrastructure as an Asset Class and Address the Information Gap*, OECD Publishing, Paris, *http://www.oecd.org/daf/fin/private-pensions/Breaking-Silos%20-Actions-to%20Develop-Infrastructure-as-an-Asset-Class-and-Address-the-Information-Gap.pdf* (accessed on 20 July 2018). [3]

OECD (2017), *Investing in Climate, Investing in Growth*, OECD Publishing, Paris, *http://dx.doi.org/10.1787/9789264273528-en*. [1]

OECD (2017), *Investment governance and the integration of environmental, social and governance factors*, OECD Publishing, Paris, *https://www.oecd.org/investment/Investment-Governance-Integration-ESG-Factors.pdf* (accessed on 13 September 2018). [32]

OECD (2017), *OECD Business and Finance Outlook 2017*, OECD Publishing, Paris, *http://dx.doi.org/10.1787/9789264274891-en*. [8]

OECD (2015), *Mapping Channels to Mobilise Institutional Investment in Sustainable Energy*, Green Finance and Investment, OECD Publishing, Paris, *http://dx.doi.org/10.1787/9789264224582-en*. [20]

One Planet Summit (2017), *Commitments*, One Planet Summit Web Portal, *https://www.oneplanetsummit.fr/en/commitments-15* (accessed on 19 October 2018). [28]

TCFD (2017), *Recommendations of the Task Force on Climate-related Financial Disclosures*, *https://www.fsb-tcfd.org/wp-content/uploads/2017/06/FINAL-TCFD-Report-062817.pdf* (accessed on 12 September 2018). [29]

UN Environment (2018), *Shifting the Lens (forthcoming)*, UN Environment, *https://www.unepinquiry.org*. [10]

UN PRI (n.d.), *About the PRI*, PRI Web Portal, *https://www.unpri.org/pri* (accessed on 19 October 2018). [12]

UNEP Inquiry (2018), "Greening the Rules of the Game: How Sustainability Factors Are Being Incorporated Into Financial Policy and Regulation", *Inquiry Working Paper*, No. 18/01, UN Environment, *http://unepinquiry.org/wp-content/uploads/2018/04/Greening_the_Rules_of_the_Game.pdf* (accessed on 13 September 2018). [6]

UNEP Inquiry (2018), *Making Waves: Aligning the Financial System with Sustainable Development*, UN Environment, Geneva, *http://unepinquiry.org/making-waves/*. [7]

UNFCCC (2017), *More than 20 Countries Launch Global Alliance to Phase Out Coal*, *https://unfccc.int/news/more-than-20-countries-launch-global-alliance-to-phase-out-coal* (accessed on 20 July 2018). [13]

Financing Climate Futures
Rethinking Infrastructure

Chapter 6

Rethink development finance for climate

Development banks and development finance institutions are major financiers of infrastructure and could play a stronger role in supporting developing countries transition to low-emission, resilient development. This chapter presents an overview of why development banks play a critical role, with a special focus on national development banks (NDBs). It discusses progress to date, as well as barriers and potential opportunities of scaling up climate finance. Three key actions are proposed for governments and the banks themselves: strengthen mandates and incentives, mobilise new investors and sources of finance to create new climate markets, and use concessional finance strategically.

Key messages

While many different actors will need to be mobilised to help address the sustainable infrastructure challenge, development banks and development finance institutions are critical, particularly in developing country contexts. But for these banks to play a transformational role, they need to do more to integrate climate into underlying development objectives, better align overall portfolios with the Paris Agreement and scale up efforts to unlock commercial investment. Development banks cannot do this alone – their activities are dependent on, and strongly influenced by, shareholder and client governments. Scaling up climate action requires governments and development banks to make three key changes:

- Strengthen development banks' mandates and incentives to deliver transformative climate action.
- Bring new investors and sources of finance to investments to create new climate markets.
- Use concessional finance to enable development banks to drive the transformation.

Why are development banks transformative?

Meeting the goals of the Paris Agreement will require all countries to reduce emissions and increase resilience to climate change. While most developing countries – especially low-income countries – are not currently a major source of emissions, they must make a decisive transition towards a climate-compatible future if they are to safeguard the significant gains made in improving human development in past decades. Poorer populations and communities are often the most vulnerable to the impacts of a changing climate, and without decisive action, increasing climate impacts could drive more than 100 million people into poverty by 2030 (Hallegatte et al., 2016[1]). Further, new work shows that climate change could induce over 143 million people from three regions – sub-Saharan Africa, South Asia, and Latin America – to migrate out of their own countries (Rigaud et al., 2018[2]).

Making a decisive transition towards climate-compatible development pathways will require developing countries to adopt inclusive development strategies, underpinned by development plans and infrastructure pipelines that consider climate change. Improving "hard" infrastructure – roads, power plants, water supply systems – is key, as is addressing "soft" infrastructure – governance and financial systems, institutions, and agriculture and forestry sectors. While many different actors will need to be mobilised to help address the challenge, development banks – publicly-owned financial institutions with a specific development or policy mandate – are critical. These institutions leverage finance from capital markets due to their strong credit ratings and the backing of their shareholder governments, and in turn provide financing to support development outcomes.

Development banks - national, regional, bilateral, multilateral - are established financers of infrastructure, and this role can be further strengthened to shift investment for low-emission, resilient infrastructure. Their value added is three-fold:

- **Financing:** Development banks provide concessional and non-concessional finance for greenfield low-emission, resilient infrastructure projects in developing countries. These projects provide a proof-of-concept for specific technologies and investments, and business models, in new markets. They also have the potential to be refinanced later in the project cycle by commercial investors.
- **Mobilising:** Development banks can attract commercial investment *directly* to projects by improving the risk-adjusted returns from renewable energy and sustainable transport projects through risk mitigation tools and approaches. They also act as intermediaries in blending finance from donor governments and investors to scale up commercial investment (OECD, 2018[3]).
- **Reforming policies and creating markets:** Development banks can also mobilise investment *indirectly* by supporting governments in reforming core climate and broader investment policies, removing specific barriers to investment, and stimulating the creation of markets to scale up climate action. They also help to shape and direct public investments by supporting governments in planning their infrastructure and developing pipelines of projects and bring these projects to bankability through targeted project development support.

Underpinning all three dimensions is the contribution that development banks make to building capacity – institutional, technical, knowledge – both for public institutions and for private market participants. For example, development banks can work with local financial intermediaries to build awareness and help develop green finance products, which in turn can help demonstrate the viability of green finance for the local market. Development banks also demonstrate and lead by example, by putting in place measures, such as climate risk screening approaches, to align overall portfolios with climate change.

What is the state of play?

Development banks have committed to going beyond business as usual and have made ambitious commitments to scale up climate action and increase their green and climate finance activities. The major multilateral development banks (MDBs) have adopted climate finance targets, committing to double or even triple the finance they provide by 2020. The latest joint report by the major MDBs estimates that these institutions committed USD 35 billion in climate finance in 2017, representing a 28% increase from 2016 (IDB et al., 2017[4]). Beyond the MDBs, members of the International Development Finance Club (IDFC) – a global network of bilateral and national development banks and finance institutions based in OECD and non-OECD countries – committed USD 173 billion in 'green' finance in 2016. This includes USD 159 billion for climate objectives (both domestic and cross-border) and USD 14 billion for other environmental objectives (IDFC, 2017[5]). Newer institutions are also committing to sustainability. The New Development Bank, which is supported by the BRICS[1] countries, aims to earmark 60% of its financing for renewable energy projects (New Development Bank, 2016[6]).

Development banks can play a critical role in solving the infrastructure challenge in developing countries. But for their support to be truly transformational, they must support countries to "leap frog" less sustainable development pathways. This will mean delivering on the climate targets and action plans to which they have committed, aligning their overall portfolios better with the goals of the Paris Agreement, scaling up efforts to mobilise commercial investment, and supporting client countries in pursuing climate-friendly development (OECD, 2017[7]).

What are the barriers and opportunities for change?

Development banks cannot deliver on this agenda alone – their activities are dependent on and strongly influenced by shareholder and client governments. Shareholder governments influence the work of bilateral development banks and MDBs through the provision of capital as well as the review of policies and projects. While the governance arrangements of national development banks (NDBs) and bilateral banks may vary, many of them are an integral part of government systems, and their mandates and activities respond directly to policy signals. Country and regional contexts also influence how ambitious development banks can be in scaling up climate action and mobilising commercial investors. For example, a lack of established pipelines of projects in developing countries, currency and foreign exchange risks, as well as the international regulatory environment around financial stability (e.g. Basel III regulations), can inhibit efforts to mobilise commercial capital for low-emission infrastructure such as renewable energy (OECD, 2018[3]; Ang, Röttgers and Burli, 2017[8]).

A more catalytic role can be played by development banks, especially in supporting developing countries, to go beyond the ambition in current Nationally Determined Contributions (NDCs) and avoid locking in emissions-intensive development. This will require governments and the banks to rethink three areas. First, all development banks will benefit from stronger mandates to act on climate, supported by enabling institutional incentive frameworks and adequate staff capacity. This will differ significantly by institution, for example, MDBs and bilateral banks are generally at a more advanced stage of integrating climate concerns into their operations than many NDBs in developing countries. Further, development banks must support countries to create enabling environments and markets and de-risk investments to attract new investors, through a greater focus on mobilisation of commercial finance. Finally, governments should encourage development banks in their efforts by allocating concessional finance strategically to enable investments with the greatest potential to achieve the Paris goals, as well as create markets and make way for more investments with less concessional terms.

6.1. Strengthen development banks' mandates and incentives to deliver transformative climate action

Do more to align portfolios with climate goals

Development banks are not a homogenous group, but include a broad range of institutions which, working in domestic or international contexts, cover a range of geographies, and provide sovereign or private financing (see Box 6.1). They also differ significantly in their levels of mainstreaming climate considerations as well as their capacity to deliver on climate actions. At a broad level, several MDBs, NDBs and bilateral development banks have joined private banks in the Climate Action in Financial Institutions Initiative and signed up to the Initiative's five voluntary principles for mainstreaming climate action, which include an emphasis on screening climate risk as well as monitoring climate impacts. At an institutional level, some banks have adopted climate-risk screening tools and approaches to help identify the risk from future climate change on projects and introduce adaptation measures into project design. These approaches are at their most advanced in MDBs, with some banks (e.g. Asian Development Bank (ADB), Inter-American Development Bank (IDB) and the World Bank) rolling these out across their operations (AFD et al., 2015[9]), but are at an early stage of adoption across most national development banks and DFIs.

Development banks are also introducing approaches to discourage emissions-intensive technologies and alternatives. EBRD and EIB, among other banks, have adopted shadow carbon prices and are using them as part of the investment decision-making process for selective projects (Hawkins and Wright, 2018[10]). Several MDBs and bilateral development banks have moved away from supporting emissions-intensive technologies such as coal, and recently, some NDBs are doing the same. For example, the Brazilian National Development Bank (BNDES) has stated it will no longer support the financing of coal power projects. Some development banks account for the carbon impact of their projects and have also incorporated climate-related indicators into their corporate scorecards. In many cases, however, they report on indicators such as greenhouse gas savings and not necessarily on the overall carbon footprints of their portfolios, which is one measure of the extent to which their operations are aligned with the goals of the Paris Agreement (OECD, 2017[7]).

Box 6.1. **Development banks play complementary roles**

MDBs – like the World Bank – and bilateral development banks – like Germany's KfW Development Bank and France's *Agence française de développement* (AFD) – are backed by strong credit ratings and the support of their shareholders. They finance public and private projects, and bring knowledge and experience from different regions. MDBs usually include both public sector and private sector operations, and sometimes these work as separate institutions e.g. the International Finance Corporation (IFC) within the World Bank Group.

Specialised "private sector" oriented bilateral development finance institution (DFIs) – like France's Proparco, the UK's CDC and the US's Overseas Private Investment Company – finance the private sector to help create markets and spur growth, and increasingly, target the engagement of commercial investors.

At a domestic level, NDBs – like the Banco Nacional de Desenvolvimento Econômico e Social (BNDES) in Brazil or the Development Bank of South Africa (DBSA) – are domestic institutions with knowledge of and connections to local markets and actors. They finance public and private projects, and supply long-term financing in local currency. Figure 6.1 provides a simplified map of development banks and DFIs.

Figure 6.1. **The scope of operations and recipients of development banks and DFIs vary**

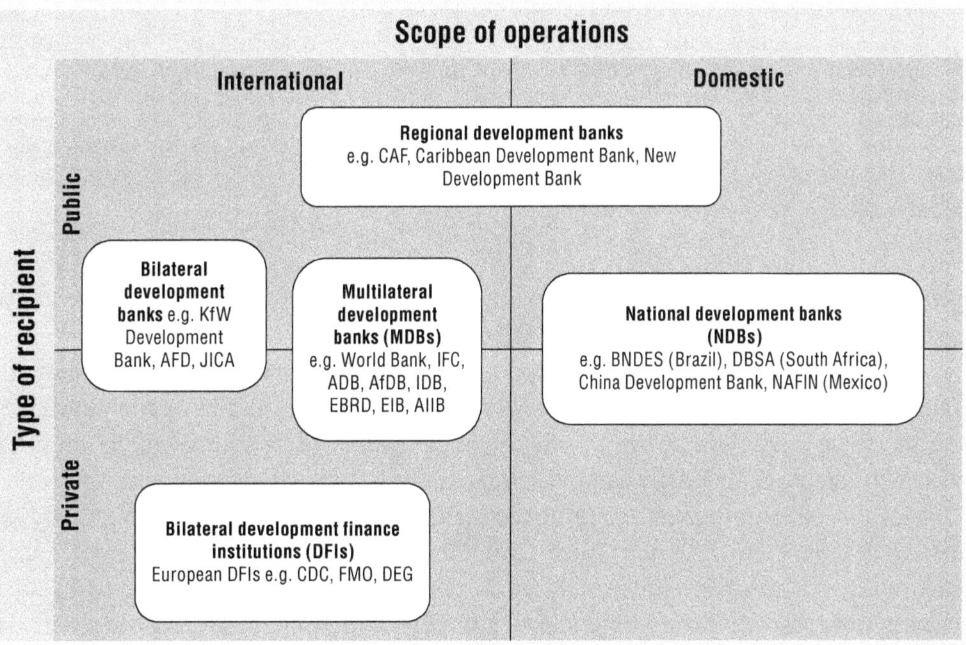

Climate targets, strategies and tools are driving increases in funds to support climate action, but there are still gaps in support for climate-compatible infrastructure, as illustrated by MDBs' support for infrastructure sectors. Based on data reported by the MDBs to the OECD Development Assistance Committee (DAC), six MDBs[2] committed USD 32.2 billion to infrastructure sectors per year, on average in 2015-16, of which USD 9.9 billion (31%) was climate-related.[3] Across infrastructure sectors, the energy sector recorded the highest share of climate-related commitments (48%) in 2015-16, with 25% of commitments to transport and 17% of commitments to water being climate-related. These figures include specifically defined climate components of projects only and therefore the share of investments that would be climate-screened would be higher. While the optimum level of mainstreaming of climate considerations will vary by sector, these figures point to a general need for more concerted action in the transport and water sectors (Figure 6.2).

Figure 6.2. **Share of MDB commitments for infrastructure that are climate-related, by sector, 2015-16 average**

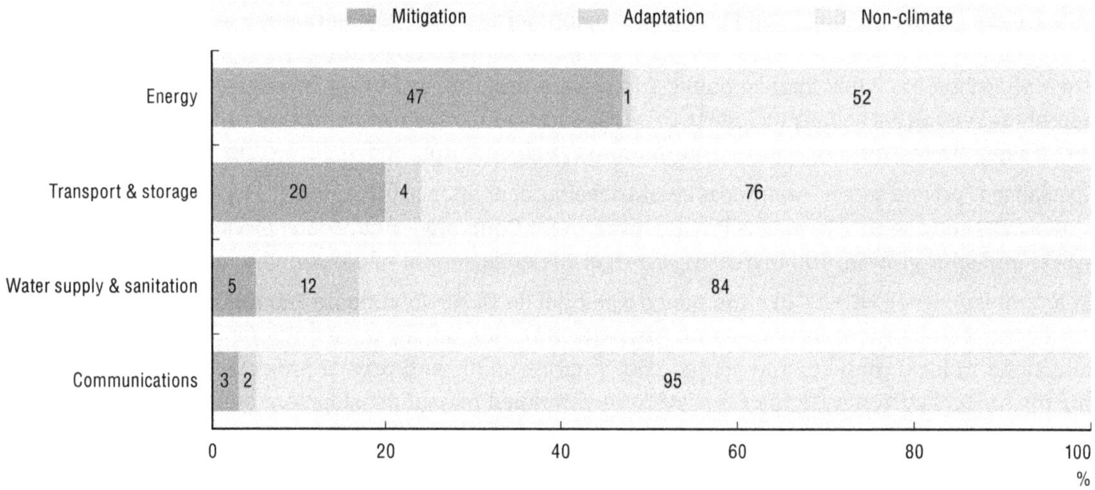

Note: This graph is based on commitment data (constant USD 2016 values) reported to the OECD DAC by the following MDBs: African Development Bank (AfDB), the Asian Development Bank (ADB), the European Bank for Reconstruction and Development (EBRD), the European Investment Bank (EIB), the Inter-American Development Bank (IDB) and the World Bank. The International Finance Corporation (IFC) is not included in this graph due to lack of data. Climate-related components of projects are those that target mitigation and adaptation, based on the joint MDB Climate Finance Tracking Methodology. MDB commitments include concessional and non-concessional support.

Source: OECD $(2017_{[11]})$, *OECD-DAC Statistical System* (database), *http://www.oecd.org/dac/financing-sustainable-development/development-finance-topics/climate-change.htm.*

StatLink https://doi.org/10.1787/888933856473

Several banks recognise the need to align their portfolios with the goals of the Paris Agreement. At the 2017 One Planet Summit, the major MDBs and IDFC committed as a group to "redirect financial flows" in support of a transition towards climate-compatible development. AFD has committed to make all their activities consistent with low-carbon and climate-resilient development and to support countries in their formulation of low-carbon and climate-resilient development trajectories ("100% Paris Agreement-compatible") (AFD, $2017_{[12]}$). Building on these commitments there is a need for more work to clarify what it means in practice to align portfolios with the goals of the Paris Agreement. As shown in Figure 6.2, the share of climate-related infrastructure commitments varies by sector. This does not mean that the remainder of the portfolios in these sectors are necessarily detrimental to the achievement of the goals of the Paris Agreement, but there is a lack of information in this area. A recent study of alignment proposes that for MDB portfolios to be truly coherent with the Paris Agreement, they should "only consist of investments that either actively support or do not undermine" the Paris temperature goal (Germanwatch and NewClimate Institute, 2018[13]). It proposes that one way for MDBs to do this would be to clearly track aligned and misaligned investments. Certainly, it is important for development banks to reduce or phase out investments in emissions-intensive technologies e.g. coal power generation.

In addition to aligning portfolios, development banks must continue to integrate climate objectives into their development goals and provide financing for infrastructure that delivers simultaneously on the Sustainable Development Goals (SDGs). For example, delivering clean energy access can be a "golden thread" for development running through all the SDGs by contributing to inclusive economic growth, greater gender equality and education, better human health and well-being, while also leading to reduced greenhouse gas emissions and improved local environments. Clean energy opportunities are available in developing countries, as illustrated by the case of energy access in sub-Saharan Africa (see Box 6.2). However, development finance for the latest and most promising technologies is still relatively limited and does not yet match the potential to take these to scale.

Box 6.2. **Decentralised solar and innovative business models can dramatically increase clean energy access in sub-Saharan Africa**

Nowhere is the imperative of clean energy access more evident than in sub-Saharan Africa, where electricity access extends to only about half of the region's population. Lack of access is a drag on the region's economic development, and the opportunity costs of chronic electricity shortages alone are estimated at 2% of annual GDP.

Social well-being is challenged by a lack of access to clean cooking, which is available to only one-third of the population. Reliance on traditional, highly polluting cooking fuels like wood, dung and charcoal carries a high human toll, harming especially women and children, and is estimated to cause a half a million premature deaths per year in sub-Saharan Africa alone.

Despite some progress, further policy and financing efforts are not keeping pace and the energy access gap is widening. The region will account for 90% of the world's population without electricity and for nearly 40% of those without clean cooking by 2030, without stepped up action (IEA, 2017[14]).

What are the barriers to expanding clean energy access?

Despite opportunities to scale up the markets for clean energy and clean cooking, many barriers remain:

- Solar household system (SHS) and Pico solar device markets are growing fast. However they could expand even more quickly with supportive commercial policies, such as measures aimed at removing import tariffs and foreign currency restrictions, or at strengthening local capital markets to attract working capital and lower the cost of doing business.
- Mini-grids require more complex infrastructure planning, enabling energy regulations, and higher levels of organisational support and investment. While they often rely on capital subsidies to be built, mini-grids do not require operating subsidies, unlike most grid systems. Mini-grid businesses with the right skill sets are emerging, but the risk-return proposition for investors is still weak and governments in many cases have been slow to reform regulations, such as tariff rules, to incentivise investments.
- Clean cooking policies are often not ambitious enough and not prioritised, leading to poor implementation and limited financing. Though women could become powerful entrepreneurial players and agents of change in this area, their role is not widely embraced in today's markets.

Box 6.2. **Decentralised solar and innovative business models can dramatically increase clean energy access in sub-Saharan Africa** *(cont.)*

Yet, the opportunity to scale up is clear. Innovative technologies and market developments, especially for solar, are dramatically expanding the number of options and lowering the costs for ensuring universal access by 2030.

What policies are required?

A major step-up in policies and financing is required, including building greater domestic capacity to utilise the needed investments and to attract new businesses.

- Official development finance (ODF) flows in the region need to be directed towards emerging clean energy access opportunities. This is especially true in areas where subsidies are needed to grow markets, i.e. mini-grids and clean cooking. Development finance actors are committing about USD 6 billion per year in ODF to the electricity sector in sub-Saharan Africa (excluding domestic and private flows). However, the majority of finance flowing to electricity today is for on-grid operations and almost no ODF flows to clean cooking (SE4ALL, 2017[15]). To expand renewable mini-grids and clean cooking businesses, there is a need to increase and leverage international ODF for blending to de-risk and attract private investment at scale. This is starting to happen, but not at the level required to bring about transformative change.
- Domestic leadership, policy reforms and greater capacity are also required to better align fiscal incentives, allow system-wide integration of decentralised renewable electricity, and help public and private investments flow. Development finance actors and governments will need to collaborate on these underpinning policies.

In the specific area of clean cooking, international public finance could play a useful role by creating an initial demand for clean cooking, and engaging women as champions of change through awareness-raising campaigns. Governments also need to work with donors to foster support behind implementation of such innovative projects.

While providing electricity access via national grids will continue to play a key role in sub-Saharan Africa, there is potential for leapfrogging traditional centralised power systems based on fossil fuels to cleaner sources.

Advances in new energy technologies (e.g. solar mini-grids, small and photovoltaic-powered devices, such as "Pico" solar lanterns, or SHSs) are already providing access to millions of users. About 4 million Pico and SHS units were sold in 2016-17, an increase of 50% in one year. These are expanding rapidly in East Africa, and are now emerging in West and Central Africa, and are already attracting commercial finance with markets buoyed by the declining cost of solar devices. These new off-grid and mini-grid options can reach people faster and in a more targeted way than grid expansion alone, and while the cost per kilowatt hour is often higher than grid-based electricity, these options come with many benefits. They are less capital intensive and offer affordable electricity services at a much lower cost than diesel alternatives, for example, providing clean, affordable electricity to unconnected rural and underserved urban populations.

For clean cooking, a range of clean cookstove and fuel opportunities also exist (e.g. from improved biomass fuels to liquified petroleum gas). While funding the supply of fuels for clean cooking may require large investments, these options can also deliver huge social and economic returns.

Source: Corfee-Morlot, J., P. Parks, J. Ogunleye and F. Ayeni (2018[16]), Achieving Clean Energy Access in Sub-Saharan Africa (forthcoming), *Financing Climate Futures Case Studies.*

Empower national development banks to play a greater role in transforming climate action

The development and climate finance landscape is changing rapidly, especially with regards to infrastructure. The relatively modest role of international development actors is highlighted clearly in the breakdown of infrastructure financing in developing countries. Miyamoto and Chiofalo (2016[17]) estimate that official development finance – from donors, MDBs and bilateral banks – makes up only 6-7% of infrastructure financing in developing countries, with most of the resources coming from national governments and a third from the private sector. Emerging economies also play a greater role than before. In 2014, for example, non-DAC countries (including many emerging economies) provided an estimated 17% of total global development co-operation finance (around USD 32 billion) with this amount being seen to increase year on year between 2010 and 2017 (Benn and Luijkx, 2017[18]).

Within this changing development finance landscape, NDBs, particularly those from emerging economies, are set to play a larger, and potentially transformational, role in scaling up finance for low-emission, resilient infrastructure in domestic contexts (see Box 6.3). NDBs are well placed to understand country-specific bottlenecks to climate investments due to their proximity to the market and relationships with local public and private actors. NDBs also provide financing in local currencies, and by adopting measures to integrate climate considerations into their lending activities, they can have a demonstration effect among other financial institutions in the country.

The potential of NDBs is highlighted more prominently in regional and national contexts. A detailed assessment of public and private climate finance for projects in South Africa between 2010 and 2015 found that national development and other public banks – like the Development Bank of South Africa (DBSA) and the Industrial Development Corporation of South Africa – played a major role, mobilising 64% of the USD 10.1 billion in private co-finance in these projects (McNicoll et al., 2017[19]). It also found that NDBs from other emerging economies (such as the China Development Bank) are also increasingly important, mobilising 17% of the private co-financing in South Africa in 2014-15. Similarly, another study focused on Latin America found that 12 domestically focused institutions in Brazil, Chile and Mexico provided USD 11 billion in climate finance in 2015 in these three countries alone, the majority of which went to infrastructure sectors, and supported the scale up of private investment (Abramskiehn et al., 2017[20]).

NDBs from emerging economies, in particular, need to be empowered by their governments and the international community to take on a stronger role in climate action. Coherent mandates and clear policy trajectories are critical for NDBs, many of which continue to support coal-related projects. In addition, many NDBs lack sufficient expertise and processes to adequately include climate considerations in their operations and may not have the capacity or the experience needed to access international climate support and scale up green financing. Targeted support could help NDBs develop and roll out climate-risk screening and other mainstreaming approaches. Despite their importance, the absence of widely adopted standards for reporting green investments amongst NDBs makes it difficult to track and assess what these banks finance. Initial inroads are being made in this area through the harmonised "Common Principles on Climate Finance Tracking", jointly established by IDFC members and MDBs, which set out definitions and guidelines for tracking climate finance and has enabled individual banks to collect information in a comparable way (AFD et al., 2015[9]). Despite this, comparable, granular information on the composition of NDB portfolios is not yet readily available (OECD, 2017[7]).

Box 6.3. **The role of emerging economy NDBs in scaling up climate-compatible infrastructure**

Among development banks, NDBs from major emerging economies such as Brazil (BNDES), China (the China Development Bank), South Africa (DBSA) and Turkey (the Industrial Development Bank of Turkey, TSKB) are rising to the forefront of international discussions on infrastructure and climate change.

Many of these banks are part of the International Development Finance Club (IDFC), a global network of 23 development banks and finance institutions, which includes emerging economy NDBs; OECD-based bilateral development banks like KfW, AFD and JICA; and subregional development banks like the Development Bank of Latin America (CAF). IDFC members committed USD 173 billion in 'green' finance in 2016, including USD 159 billion in climate finance and USD 14 billion in finance for other environmental objectives. The major share of this finance stemmed from institutions based in non-OECD countries, and supported domestic projects. The remainder – USD 26 billion – went towards financing projects in other countries. While much of this cross-border financing originated in banks in OECD countries, USD 7 billion was committed by IDFC members based outside the OECD for other developing countries, highlighting the growing role of emerging economy banks in international environment-related development finance.

The case of two banks – BNDES in Brazil and DBSA in South Africa – highlights the role NDBs already play in their national contexts and their support for low-emission, climate-resilient infrastructure.

Both banks are important actors in the context of national economic development and infrastructure.

BNDES is one of the largest development banks in the world, with total assets estimated at 13% of GDP in 2017, and has played a major role in financing infrastructure in Brazil. DBSA is one of three NDBs in South Africa, has a strong focus on infrastructure development, and increasingly works outside of South Africa to support infrastructure development in other countries in the Southern African Development Community.

BNDES and DBSA already support the deployment of low-emission infrastructure in their countries.

As the government's main instrument of long-term finance, BNDES is often implicitly a key implementer of government policy and plans on the environment. For example, BNDES manages the Amazon Fund, Brazil's main REDD+ financing mechanism, and has supported the development of Brazil's wind industry by financing wind power across the country. The bank has also maintained or increased its green economy-related financing in recent years, despite a decrease in overall disbursements.

Similarly, DBSA has played an important role in supporting South Africa's transition to a green economy through the management of the Department of Environmental Affairs-funded Green Fund, and is accredited under the Green Climate Fund (GCF) and the Global Environment Facility (GEF). DBSA's support for the setup of South Africa's Renewable Energy Independent Power Producer Procurement Programme and subsequent financing for projects within the programme highlights its role as a key player in the roll-out of the government's renewable energy plans.

Transitioning from "financer" to "mobiliser" of investment for infrastructure

Spurred by national awareness of the limitations in public finance and the need for more infrastructure investment, both BNDES and DBSA are transitioning from their traditional role as providers of long-term finance for infrastructure to enablers and mobilisers of other sources of finance.

DBSA has clearly recognised the importance of this transition, and has recently adopted a corporate target and is reporting on finance catalysed as a result of their operations, alongside original measures of disbursement and portfolio size. The bank's proposed Climate Finance Facility, recently approved for financing from the GCF, is an example of how DBSA can support the mobilisation of commercial finance. The facility is based on a blended finance structure that will crowd in commercial capital by improving the risk-return profile of commercially viable climate projects in local currency that are not able to self-fund in the market.

Box 6.3. **The role of emerging economy NDBs in scaling up climate-compatible infrastructure** *(cont.)*

BNDES's new mission recognises the importance of its ongoing work on capital markets development. In May 2017, BNDES issued a USD 1 billion green bond which was the first international green bond issuance by a Brazilian bank. Another example, is the bank's BRL 500 million Sustainable Energy Fund (*Fundo de Energia Sustentável*), which builds on an established securitisation framework to finance the construction of sustainable energy projects and securitise the less risky operational phase of sustainable energy projects.

Source: OECD (2018[21]), Mobilising commercial capital for sustainable infrastructure: Insights from national development banks in Brazil and South Africa (forthcoming), *Financing Climate Futures Case Studies*; IDFC (2017[5]), *IDFC Green Finance Mapping Report 2016*, International Development Finance Club (IDFC).

Strengthen mandates, incentives and capacity

Shareholder governments need to give development banks stronger, more coherent mandates to deliver transformative climate action by integrating climate with underlying development objectives, reflecting this in corporate scorecards, and putting in place supportive internal incentive systems to encourage staff to scale up climate action. Incentive structures in development banks need to reflect sustainability outcomes alongside financial targets. Corporate and staff performance in some institutions, and unless otherwise managed, can be driven more by financial indicators (e.g. commitments or disbursements) than by efforts to mobilise commercial finance, or the potential contribution to development outcomes such as climate change (Bhattacharya et al., 2018[22]). This encourages an emphasis by institutions and individual officers on larger investments, especially in infrastructure, but does not necessarily encourage investments in areas such as energy efficiency or distributed renewable energy where the ticket sizes could be smaller but which are critical for reducing emissions and building resilience. The example of sub-Saharan Africa, which faces gaps in development finance for distributed renewable technologies, illustrates this (see Box 6.2). Some development banks resolve this by working with financial intermediaries, for example in the case of energy efficiency credit lines.

Development banks also need to have adequate capacity and skills to scale up transformational action on climate change. They need to dedicate efforts to "non-traditional" areas (i.e. investment models that support the financing of new technologies and programmatic approaches centred on climate change), and avoid a bias towards more traditional infrastructure projects when assessing investment opportunities. While bilateral and multilateral development banks are beginning to build these skills in country and sector departments, many NDBs in developing countries still face significant capacity gaps in these areas. Often multilateral and bilateral development banks also work with NDBs to build their capacity. For example, IDB has set up the Green Finance in Latin America and the Caribbean platform, which supports NDBs to exchange knowledge and scale up green financing products and approaches.[4]

6.2. Bring new investors and sources of finance to investments to create new climate markets

The investment gap for infrastructure, especially in developing countries, highlights the need for scarce public resources to be used strategically to attract commercial investment, where suitable. As a result, the links between private finance and development finance are getting closer, with many private finance actors embracing the Environmental, Social and Governance (ESG) agenda, and with more pressure on development banks and development finance institutions to work closely with commercial actors. This convergence is particularly prominent in impact investing, an emerging area where private investors and development finance institutions work side-by-side to support projects that have a measurable environmental or social impact as well as produce financial returns (Wilson, 2016[23]).

Development banks are beginning to make headway in mobilising private climate investments. At the international level, development finance institutions – such as IFC and the European DFIs – directly engage with and finance private businesses and local banks in developing countries. They can facilitate investors' involvement in climate-related investment by, for example, pooling small-scale projects together and raising finance through green bonds. Blended finance – the use of development finance to mobilise commercial support for development projects – is also increasing among development banks and DFIs (OECD, 2018[3]). Development banks use a range of risk mitigation instruments (such as guarantees), mezzanine financing and syndication to attract commercial investment to low-emission infrastructure projects. In many cases, concessional finance from donor and climate funds is used in conjunction with development bank financing to provide senior debt with longer tenors or concessional interest rates to help bridge the viability gap for climate-related investments. One innovative approach to attract commercial investment is the use of subordinated capital in structured blended funds. The EIB-managed Global Energy Efficiency and Renewable Energy Fund (GEEREF), for example, uses a blended capital structure to attract commercial investors, investing capital in specialist renewable energy private equity funds which in turn support greenfield renewable energy projects, through a 'fund of funds' model (OECD, 2018[3]).

While these approaches are gaining traction, they are still only a small part of what development banks do. A much stronger focus on mobilising commercial investment is needed and will require banks to re-envision the way in which they finance development. This message is also echoed by the G20 Eminent Persons Group on Global Financial Governance (see Box 6.4), and is illustrated in the World Bank's "Cascade approach". It sets out a path for the bank to "maximise financing for development", guiding bank staff to prioritise opportunities to draw on private finance for development outcomes where appropriate, and reserve scarce public financing for those areas where private sector engagement may not be feasible (World Bank Group, 2017[24]). It also scales up bank support to improve the enabling environment for private investment. A concrete illustration of this approach is the Private Sector Window that has been created as part of the replenishment of the World Bank's International Development Association (IDA) which supports the world's poorest countries, and many fragile and conflict-affected states. This window represents a significant step forward in actively supporting public-private solutions in these countries (IDA, 2017[25]). Jointly, MDBs have also signed up to the G20 Hamburg Principles for crowding-in private finance, which similarly take a step wise approach to mobilising commercial finance, first focusing on the investment enabling environment and then encouraging the prioritisation of commercial finance, where appropriate (G20 IFA WG, 2017[26]).

In order to implement this vision, there will need to be a much stronger focus on bringing new investors and sources of finance with the explicit aim of creating new climate markets. This means working with governments to develop enabling policies and regulations to scale up commercial investment, optimising the risks that development banks carry, and using concessional finance – through blended finance, for example – in cases where investments are critical to achieve climate goals, but cannot be viably financed through non-concessional windows.

Box 6.4. **G20 Eminent Persons Group: A greater focus on mobilising private capital for development impact is central to proposed reforms for global financial governance**

The G20 Eminent Persons Group on Global Financial Governance (EPG) was tasked by G20 Finance Ministers and Central Bank Governors to review global financial architecture and the current system of governance of International Financial Institutions (IFIs). The purpose of this review was to propose reforms that the G20 could take forward to better support sustainability in a changing global context.

The EPG's report to the G20 was released in October 2018, and includes 22 proposed reforms focused on three areas: increasing collaboration to achieve development impact, improving the resilience of the global financial system, and improving the way the G20 and IFIs work. Central to these proposals is the recognition that a much greater focus is needed on domestic resource mobilisation as well as on mobilising private investment in order to solve development challenges.

The report suggests that development finance needs to be re-oriented to focus on reducing and managing risk so as to mobilise capital at scale, including through a greater focus on securitisation and better risk insurance. In particular, the EPG's fourth proposal is to "Reduce and diversify risk on a system-wide basis to mobilise significantly greater private investment, including portfolio-based infrastructure financing". It suggests that to achieve this, the G20 must:

- "Shift the basic business model of the MDBs from direct lending towards risk mitigation aimed at mobilising private capital";
- Put in place "system-wide political risk insurance"; and
- "Build a developing country infrastructure asset class" to attract institutional investors.

Source: G20 Eminent Persons Group on Global Financial Governance (2018[27]), *Making the Global Financial System Work for All.*

This could be encouraged through a greater emphasis on the crowding-in of private commercial finance, where this is possible and relevant, in corporate scorecards (Blended Finance Taskforce, 2017[28]). However, while the use of "leverage ratios" is a helpful metric used in annual reports to highlight the volumes of finance crowded in, they need to be dynamic, reflecting changes in country contexts (e.g. rapidly falling costs of renewable energy over time). At the same time, the development banks and DFIs must have in place clear exit strategies to avoid eventual crowding out of commercial capital (OECD, 2017[29]). In addition, indirect efforts to mobilise commercial finance – such as support towards enabling environments – are not captured well in most current efforts to measure mobilisation, and too great a focus on leverage ratios could disincentivise these much-needed efforts (McNicoll et al., 2017[19]). Developing agreed metrics to track indirect mobilisation could help incentivise these efforts and monitor future progress. It is also important to ensure that measures to mobilise commercial finance are well aligned with climate goals.

While there are no "silver bullets" that can overcome the array of barriers to mobilising commercial investment for low-emission, climate-resilient infrastructure at scale, development banks and other stakeholders, working together, can help resolve major bottlenecks and build the much-needed project pipelines in developing countries by:

- **Intermediating and aggregating smaller investments** through, for example, structured blended finance vehicles, to help bridge the mismatch between the nature of the demand side of financing for projects and the nature of supply of financing from financial markets, and to bring in institutional investors.
- **Standardising the terms and conditions related to low-emission infrastructure projects** to help unlock private investment, including those underpinning different instruments, approaches and contractual agreements. One recent example is the TerraWatt Initiative, which brings together development banks and other finance institutions, legal firms and associations to compile open source contracts and guidelines for solar energy in an effort to bring down related transaction costs (TerraWatt Initiative[30]).
- Deploying risk mitigation measures, including efforts to **effectively manage currency risks**, which are critical for channeling investment towards developing countries. More effective pooling of resources and collective risk management could help reduce the cost of providing long-term finance in local currency.

6.3. Use concessional finance strategically to enable development banks to drive the transformation

Governments – and the capital as well as the concessional finance that they provide – are important direct and indirect drivers of change among development banks. Financing from NDBs reflects the policy directions of their government, and can, in many cases, support investments in pollution, emission-intensive investments. The China Development Bank, for example, is rapidly scaling up green finance, but continues to support coal, as does DBSA (OECD, 2017[7]).

Amongst the MDBs, shareholders directly influence environmental performance and guide activities and operations, usually engaging at a strategic level (when reviewing or updating policies) and at an operational level (when approving projects) (Crishna Morgado and Taskin, 2018[31]). They also provide capital and concessional finance to support targeted operations. The recent capital increase for the World Bank Group, for example, clearly encourages the bank's approach to actively crowd in private resources as well as its support for climate change and other global public goods (World Bank, 2018[32]). Governments also use external policy channels to give policy directions to development banks – for example, in the case of Italy's G7 Presidency and Germany's G20 Presidency in 2017.[5]

As shareholders and investors in development banks and development finance institutions, governments must make greater efforts to provide clear, coherent signals and guidance to take a stronger role in driving transformative climate investments. Amidst demands for support on a variety of development challenges, development banks' efforts to mobilise private capital for sustainable infrastructure are dependent both on their own balance sheet and lending capacity, as well as on concessional finance from donors. The latter is key to help bridge viability gaps for investments in countries where markets are maturing and are not yet optimal for mobilising commercial finance purely at market terms (Trabacchi et al., 2016[33]).

Targeted, concessional finance for climate action – provided bilaterally from governments as well as through multilateral climate funds – can help development banks make the case for climate-related investments to client countries and institutions that are not yet actively seeking such investments. Importantly, the changing climate finance architecture, including the scale down of the Climate Investment Funds and the operationalisation of the Green Climate Fund, has implications for how NDBs, MDBs and bilateral DFIs access concessional finance. To continue to encourage development banks to help developing countries transform their development pathways, governments should ensure there is adequate concessional financing available, and that it is allocated to investments which have the potential to create markets and make way for more investments at less concessional terms, e.g. by creating scale or serving as proof-of-concept for newer approaches. New work in this area suggests that climate finance should be prioritised based on two factors: the level of ambition (i.e. contribution to the Paris goals) and the potential for transformation (i.e. the degree to which it could reduce barriers to future climate investments). In addition, the level of concessionality of climate finance should be proportionate to the effort required to make it viable (World Bank, 2018[34]).

Concessional finance – through blended finance – is also key to increase the viability of public and private investments in countries where markets are not yet optimal for mobilising commercial finance purely at market terms. An example of this is the Canadian Climate Fund for the Private Sector in Asia, managed by ADB, which uses concessional finance to support private sector projects with a high climate impact but that were unlikely to have proceeded on a commercial basis alone (ADB[35]). This support needs to be well-targeted and efficiently allocated to help make projects viable. Its use in mobilising private finance should be underpinned by strong policy principles and standards to ensure that the focus is on crowding in investment without distorting markets (OECD, 2018[3]). MDBs and bilateral DFIs have agreed on joint principles to govern the use of concessional finance in private sector operations, emphasising issues such as additionality, minimising concessionality, the importance of reinforcing markets and for underpinning these investments with robust ESG standards (IFC, 2017[36]).

Notes

1. A group of five large emerging economies composed of Brazil, the Russian Federation, India, the People's Republic of China and South Africa.
2. Including the Asian Development Bank (ADB), the African Development Bank (AfDB), the European Investment Bank (EIB), the European Bank for Reconstruction and Development (EBRD), the Inter-American Development Bank (IDB) and the World Bank – excluding the International Finance Corporation (IFC).
3. This is based on data reported to the OECD DAC by the MDBs. MDBs report activity level development finance data as well as climate-related activity level data to the OECD DAC. Climate-related data includes climate co-benefits i.e. climate-related components of projects (i.e. those that target mitigation, adaptation, or both mitigation and adaptation) and is based on the joint MDB Climate Finance Tracking Methodology.
4. For more information: *https://www.greenfinancelac.org/*
5. Italy's G7 Presidency supported a discussion on the alignment of MDB portfolios with the Paris Agreement, and the Hamburg Climate and Energy Action Plan under Germany's G20 Presidency called on MDBs to deliver scaled up climate action.

References

Abramskiehn, D. et al. (2017), *Supporting National Development Banks to Drive Investment in the Nationally Determined Contributions of Brazil, Mexico, and Chile*, Inter-American Development Bank (IDB), Washington, DC, *https://publications.iadb.org/bitstream/handle/11319/8520/Supporting-National-Development-Banks-to-Drive-Investment-in-the-Nationally-Determined-Contributions-of-Brazil-Mexico-and-Chile.PDF* (accessed on 19 October 2018). [20]

ADB (n.d.), *Canadian Climate Fund for the Private Sector in Asia*, Asian Development Bank Web Portal, *https://www.adb.org/site/funds/funds/canadian-climate-fund-for-the-private-sector-in-asia* (accessed on 19 October 2018). [35]

AFD (2017), *Climate and Development Strategy 2017-2022*, Agence française de développement, Paris, *https://www.afd.fr/sites/afd/files/2017-12/climate-development-strategy-2017-2022.pdf* (accessed on 19 October 2018). [12]

AFD et al. (2015), *Mainstreaming Climate Action within Financial Institutions: Emerging Practices*, *https://www.mainstreamingclimate.org/wp-content/uploads/2017/03/fi_mainstreaming_epp_en-1.pdf* (accessed on 19 October 2018). [9]

Ang, G., D. Röttgers and P. Burli (2017), "The empirics of enabling investment and innovation in renewable energy", *OECD Environment Working Papers*, No. 123, OECD Publishing, Paris, *http://dx.doi.org/10.1787/67d221b8-en*. [8]

Benn, J. and W. Luijkx (2017), "Emerging providers' international co-operation for development", *OECD Development Co-operation Working Papers*, No. 33, OECD Publishing, Paris, *https://doi.org/10.1787/15d6a3c7-en* (accessed on 19 October 2018). [18]

Bhattacharya, A. et al. (2018), *The New Global Agenda and the Future of the Multilateral Development Bank System*, Brookings Institution, Center for Global Development and Overseas Development Institute (ODI), *https://www.brookings.edu/wp-content/uploads/2018/02/epg_paper_on_future_of_mdb_system_jan30.pdf* (accessed on 19 October 2018). [22]

Blended Finance Taskforce (2017), *Better Finance, Better World: Consultation Paper of the Blended Finance Taskforce*, Business and Sustainable Development Commission (Blended Finance Taskforce), London, *http://s3.amazonaws.com/aws-bsdc/BFT_BetterFinance_final_01192018.pdf* (accessed on 19 October 2018). [28]

Corfee-Morlot, J. et al. (2018), "Achieving Clean Energy Access in Sub-Saharan (forthcoming)", *Financing Climate Futures Case Studies*, 3CS and Carbon Limits Nigeria, Paris. [16]

Crishna Morgado, N. and Ö. Taskin (2018), "Managing environmental risks in development banks and development finance institutions: What role for donor shareholders? (forthcoming)", *OECD Development Co-operation Working Papers*, OECD Publishing, Paris, *https://doi.org/10.1787/22220518* (accessed on 19 October 2018). [31]

G20 Eminent Persons Group on Global Financial Governance (2018), *Making the Global Financial System Work for All*, *https://www.globalfinancialgovernance.org/assets/pdf/G20EPG-Full%20Report.pdf* (accessed on 26 October 2018). [27]

G20 IFA WG (2017), *Principles of MDBs' strategy for crowding-in Private Sector Finance for growth and sustainable development*, G20 International Financial Architecture Working Group, *https://www.bundesfinanzministerium.de/Content/DE/Downloads/G20-Dokumente/principles-on-crowding-in-private-sector-finance-april-20.pdf?__blob=publicationFile&v=2* (accessed on 19 October 2018). [26]

Germanwatch and NewClimate Institute (2018), *Aligning Investments with the Paris Agreement Temperature Goal: Challenges and Opportunities for Multilateral Development Banks*, Germanwatch and NewClimate Institute, *https://newclimate.org/wp-content/uploads/2018/09/MDB_WorkingPaper_2018-09.pdf* (accessed on 19 October 2018). [13]

Hallegatte, S. et al. (2016), *Shock Waves: Climate Change and Development Series Managing the Impacts of Climate Change on Poverty*, The World Bank, Washington, DC, *https://openknowledge.worldbank.org/bitstream/handle/10986/22787/9781464806735.pdf* (accessed on 27 September 2018). [1]

Hawkins, J. and H. Wright (2018), *How are development banks performing on shadow carbon pricing?*, E3G Web Portal, *https://www.e3g.org/library/how-are-development-banks-performing-on-shadow-carbon-pricing* (accessed on 19 October 2018). [10]

IDA (2017), *What is the IDA18 IFC-MIGA Private Sector Window?*, International Development Association (IDA), World Bank, *https://ida.worldbank.org/sites/default/files/pdfs/ida-psw-brief-may-2017.pdf* (accessed on 19 October 2018). [25]

IDB et al. (2017), *2016 Joint Report On Multilateral Development Banks' Climate Finance*, *http://dx.doi.org/10.18235/0000806*. [4]

IDFC (2017), *IDFC Green Finance Mapping Report 2016*, International Development Finance Club, *https://www.idfc.org/Downloads/Publications/01_green_finance_mappings/IDFC_Green_Finance_Mapping_Report_2017_12_11.pdf* (accessed on 19 October 2018). [5]

IEA (2017), *Energy Access Outlook 2017: From Poverty to Prosperity*, International Energy Agency, Paris, *https://www.iea.org/publications/freepublications/publication/WEO2017SpecialReport_EnergyAccessOutlook.pdf* (accessed on 05 July 2018). [14]

IFC (2017), *DFI Working Group on Blended Concessional Finance for Private Sector Projects: Summary Report*, International Finance Corporation (IFC), World Bank Group, *https://www.ifc.org/wps/wcm/connect/30635fde-1c38-42af-97b9-2304e962fc85/DFI+Blended+Concessional+Finance+for+Private+Sector+Operations_Summary+R....pdf?MOD=AJPERES* (accessed on 19 October 2018). [36]

McNicoll, L. et al. (2017), "Estimating Publicly-Mobilised Private Finance for Climate Action: A South African Case Study", *OECD Environment Working Papers*, No. 125, OECD Publishing, Paris, *https://doi.org/10.1787/a606277c-en* (accessed on 19 October 2018). [19]

Miyamoto, K. and E. Chiofalo (2016), "Official Development Finance for Infrastructure: With a Special Focus on Multilateral Development Banks", *OECD Development Co-operation Working Papers*, No. 30, OECD Publishing, Paris, *http://dx.doi.org/10.1787/9e93790e-en*. [17]

New Development Bank (2016), *NDB President: 60% of Funding Will be for Renewables - New Development Bank*, New Development Bank Web Portal, *https://www.ndb.int/president_desk/ndb-president-60-funding-will-renewables/* (accessed on 19 October 2018). [6]

OECD (2018), *Making Blended Finance Work for the Sustainable Development Goals*, OECD Publishing, Paris, *http://dx.doi.org/10.1787/9789264288768-en*. [3]

OECD (2018), "Mobilising commercial capital for sustainable infrastructure: Insights from national development banks in Brazil and South Africa (forthcoming)", *Financing Climate Futures Case Studies*, OECD Publishing, Paris. [21]

OECD (2017), *Investing in Climate, Investing in Growth*, OECD Publishing, Paris, *http://dx.doi.org/10.1787/9789264273528-en*. [7]

OECD (2017), *OECD DAC Blended Finance Principles for Unlocking Commercial Finance for the Sustainable Development Goals*, OECD Publishing, Paris, *http://www.oecd.org/dac/financing-sustainable-development/development-finance-topics/OECD-Blended-Finance-Principles.pdf* (accessed on 19 October 2018). [29]

OECD (2017), *OECD-DAC Statistical System (database)*, *http://www.oecd.org/dac/financing-sustainable-development/development-finance-topics/climate-change.htm* (accessed on 26 October 2018). [11]

Rigaud, K. et al. (2018), *Groundswell: Preparing for Internal Climate Migration*, World Bank, Washington, DC, *http://hdl.handle.net/10986/29461* (accessed on 19 October 2018). [2]

SE4ALL (2017), *Energizing Finance: Scaling and Refining Finance In Countries With Large Energy Access Gaps*, Sustainable Energy for All, *https://www.seforall.org/sites/default/files/2017_SEforALL_FR4_PolicyPaper.pdf* (accessed on 26 July 2018). [15]

TerraWatt Initiative (n.d.), *The Global Solar Energy Standardisation Initiative*, TerraWatt Initiative Web Portal, *https://sesi.terrawatt.org/* (accessed on 19 October 2018). [30]

Trabacchi, C. et al. (2016), *The role of the Climate Investment Funds in meeting investment needs*, Climate Policy Initiative, *http://climatepolicyinitiative.org/wp-content/uploads/2016/06/The-role-of-the-Climate-Investment-Funds-in-meeting-investment-needs.pdf* (accessed on 19 October 2018). [33]

Wilson, K. (2016), *Investing for social impact in developing countries*, OECD Publishing, Paris, *http://dx.doi.org/10.1787/dcr-2016-en*. [23]

World Bank (2018), *Strategic Use of Climate Finance to Maximize Climate Action: A Guiding Framework*, World Bank Group, Washington, DC, *http://documents.worldbank.org/curated/en/879251537779825585/Strategic-Use-of-Climate-Finance-to-Maximize-Climate-Action-A-Guiding-Framework* (accessed on 19 October 2018). [34]

World Bank (2018), *World Bank/IMF Spring Meetings 2018: Development Committee Communiqué*, *http://www.worldbank.org/en/news/press-release/2018/04/21/world-bankimf-spring-meetings-2018-development-committee-communique* (accessed on 26 July 2018). [32]

World Bank Group (2017), "Maximizing Finance for Development: Leveraging the Private Sector for Growth and Sustainable Development", *http://siteresources.worldbank.org/DEVCOMMINT/Documentation/23758671/DC2017-0009_Maximizing_8-19.pdf* (accessed on 05 July 2018). [24]

Financing Climate Futures
Rethinking Infrastructure

Chapter 7

Empower city governments to build low-emission and resilient urban societies

Cities are a priority area for furthering low-emission, resilient and inclusive development. The way cities expand and develop will impact the trajectory of global emissions. Cities, especially in developing countres, are vulnerable to climate risks. This chapter explores the barriers facing cities as they grapple with the challenges of insufficient financing and infrastructure deficits, and the important development opportunities presented by financing low-emission, resilient infrastructure. The chapter describes four key actions for governments to empower cities: integrate land-use and transport policies, align national and local fiscal regulations with investment needs in cities, build climate-related and project finance capacity in cities, and seize the development benefits of low-emission, resilient planning.

Key messages

Empowering local and city governments to plan and finance low-emission, resilient infrastructure is an essential part of achieving climate and development goals. The way cities expand and develop will determine the emissions of 70% of the world's population in 2050. Cities are particularly vulnerable to climate risks and must develop strategies that ensure urban resilience. The failure to invest in the right urban forms will put residents, the local economy and social cohesion at risk, potentially exacerbating existing inequalities. National and local governments should work together to pursue the following transformative actions:

- Rethink institutional configurations to integrate land-use and transport strategies and seize the immediate development benefits of low-emission, resilient planning.
- Align national and local fiscal policies to encourage and enable low-emission, resilient investments and behaviours.
- Build climate-related and project finance capacity in cities to efficiently finance and deliver complex low-emission, resilient infrastructure projects.
- Seize the social and economic benefits of low-emission, resilient planning to deliver inclusive urban growth.

Why is action in cities transformative?

Cities are home to over half of the global population (UNDESA, 2018[1]) and account for over 80% of global GDP (UN-Habitat, 2016[2]). However, they also account for between 60 and 80% of global energy consumption and 70% of global greenhouse gas emissions (UN-Habitat, 2016[2]). As urban populations are expected to account for over 70% of the world population by 2050, trillions of dollars will be needed to expand and renew urban infrastructure. The choices made today about the types, features and location of long-lived infrastructure can play a major role in limiting the extent of climate change, contributing to the resilience of urban societies, and creating the backbone for strong, inclusive urban development.

The failure to invest in low-emission, resilient urban forms will put residents, the local economy and social cohesion at risk. Climate change threatens to exacerbate cities' existing economic and social inequalities. Low-income populations living in urban areas are vulnerable to climate change, as they tend to live in at-risk neighbourhoods (for instance, areas prone to flooding or landslides), or in poorly designed homes (such as underground apartments or informal structures). Their limited access to social insurance and safety nets further complicates recovery from climate-related incidents. Furthermore, municipalities with a high climate risk profile may be less attractive places to live and do business, and therefore potentially less economically productive (OECD, 2010[3]).

What is the state of play?

In general, urban forms are not developing in a sustainable fashion. In most OECD countries, urban sprawl has increased since 1990. Specifically, cities have become more fragmented and the share of land allocated to very low-density areas has increased. Urban areas have become denser on average, but 60% of urban space is sparsely populated (OECD, 2018[4]). Urban sprawl is driving many challenges facing cities today, including traffic congestion, air pollution, longer commuting times, reduced access to affordable housing, and increasing per-user costs of public services such as water, energy and public transport. It also contributes to many environmental challenges, including increased greenhouse gas emissions, harm to biodiversity and loss of environmental amenities.

In a business-as-usual scenario, emissions in large cities are projected to increase by 26% to 2050, partly driven by rising car use in certain regions (ITF, 2017[5]). Car use in Asia, for example, is expected to increase by 50% by 2050. Established cities are already struggling with air pollution that is consistently higher than accepted limits. Traffic congestion is also tremendously costly. For example, one study calculated that traffic congestion in Germany, the United Kingdom and the United States cost these economies a combined USD 461 billion in 2017, or USD 971 per person (INRIX, 2017[6]). Outdoor air pollution – of which a major contributor is traffic pollution – is projected to contribute to 6-9 million premature deaths a year globally, and to cost 1% of global GDP by 2060 in the absence of more stringent policies (OECD, 2016[7]).

Cities are also particularly vulnerable to climate risks and must therefore carefully craft strategies to ensure that investments made today do not become tomorrow's damaged or stranded assets. In 2014, 89% of cities – home to 2.1 billion people – were located in areas that are highly vulnerable to economic losses from natural disasters (UNDESA, 2015[8]). Extreme weather events can be particularly disruptive to complex urban systems and areas of high population density. Much of the world's urban population inhabits low-lying coastal areas, making them more vulnerable to storm surges and rising sea levels. Many of these low-lying urban areas are also rapidly expanding, which compounds risks. Cities in developing countries are particularly vulnerable to flood risks, as they are relatively less equipped to prepare for and address the fallout from disasters (Hallegatte et al., 2013[9]).

What are the barriers and opportunities for change?

Local governments have a central role to play in getting the low-emission, resilient transformation right. They often have authority over many of the decisions that matter for limiting greenhouse gas emissions and strengthening the adaptive capacity of cities, such as spatial planning and zoning, regulation of transport, building construction, water and emergency management systems (Hallegatte et al., 2016[10]).

Local governments are also major spenders and investors. Their budgets account for an increasing share of public expenditures, accounting for 40% of total public spending on average in the OECD and 57% of public investment in 2016 (OECD, 2018[11]). The nature of urban infrastructure is fundamental. Making cities more compact and connected can lower investment requirements by as much as 10% (New Climate Economy, 2014[12]), worth up to USD 17 trillion in economic savings by 2050 (New Climate Economy, 2018[13]).

Action at the local level can also result in significant economic benefits and greater social inclusion. For example, more accessible forms of transportation can help vulnerable populations participate in the workforce by increasing access to jobs (OECD, 2018[14]). Investing in climate-resilient infrastructure is therefore not only a tremendous opportunity for cities. It is also an imperative to ensure their sustainability in the context of a changing climate, to drastically reduce their emissions, and to reduce and prevent further inequalities within and between regions (see 7.1).

Despite these opportunities, cities report financing constraints in meeting their infrastructure needs (OECD, 2018[11]). There are significant barriers to cities' ability to access finance; for example, cities and subnational governments can be limited in their ability to raise revenues through taxation, and in their ability to borrow. Their capacity for long-term infrastructure planning can also be limited, particularly in smaller municipalities.

Changing the current allocation of investments and patterns of infrastructure will be challenging for even the most advanced countries and cities. It will require a better organisation of urban landscapes through the integration of land-use and transport planning policies, and a "managed" transition towards low-emission activities, the supply and uptake of low-emission technologies, and a sufficient degree of public support for this transition. For many industrial cities, this may require developing strategies to support the reorientation of existing industries in order to increase their efficiency and lessen dependence on fossil fuels. Clear communication and consultation with the public will be needed to increase awareness of the opportunities that are generated by the transition, not just the costs.

Box 7.1. **The economic and social benefits of low-emission cities**

A study by the Coalition for Urban Transition finds that the transition to low-emission cities is good for the local economy and well-being:

- Directing investment towards clean public transport and greater vehicle efficiency could create up to 23 million additional jobs a year and tackle congestion, cutting the wasted hours spent sitting in traffic by up to 30%. It could reduce by over 80% the 1.3 million transport-related deaths and 78 million transport-related injuries worldwide each year.
- Investing in city cycling infrastructure could save five times the cost of this investment by improving public health and reducing traffic congestion. Extrapolating across Europe, the health benefits from cycling could be worth USD 35-136 billion annually.
- Investing in energy efficiency for new and existing buildings could create up to 16 million additional jobs a year worldwide. Improved working and home environments would lower rates of illness, saving on health bills and making workers up to 16% more productive.

Importantly, these initiatives benefit the poor the most. Low-income groups are more likely to live in poorly-insulated buildings and neighbourhoods with chronic air pollution, and depend on public transport, cycling and walking over private car use. An ambitious programme to reduce greenhouse gas emissions would especially improve the living conditions of the poor, and therefore help to achieve more equitable cities.

Source: Andy Gouldson et al. (2018[15]), *The Economic and Social Benefits of Low-Carbon Cities: A Systematic Review of the Evidence*, Coalition for Urban Transitions, London and Washington, DC, *http://newclimateeconomy.net/content/cities-working-papers*

7.1. Integrate land-use and transport policies

The way in which cities are designed and built is a key aspect of sustainability. Infrastructure investment must therefore be integrated with land-use and transport planning. Urban forms influence the need for infrastructure, as denser developments can reduce the extent of infrastructure networks required to deliver services such as transport, water and sewage. In fast-growing cities, mainly in developing countries, where most infrastructure is being built, urban layouts – and therefore emissions pathways – are being determined now. Over 60% of the land that will be urbanised by 2030 has yet to be developed (New Climate Economy, 2018[13]). This implies a tremendous opportunity to make the "right" decisions to pursue low-emission, resilient infrastructure pathways. Acting now is crucial: it is extremely difficult and often costly to revise cityscapes once roads, houses, parking, transit ways, parks and other urban infrastructure have been built.

Box 7.2. **Sustainable cooling can have significant decarbonisation effects**

Cooling technologies are critical across virtually all sectors of society, including food, building, health, industry, data centres and transport. While cooling is often associated with comfort air conditioning, it is directly linked to essential daily economic and social needs that underpin poverty eradication and meeting the Sustainable Development Goals (SDGs). 1.1 billion people globally face immediate risks from lack of access to cooling (SE4All, 2018[16]).

In addition to being a critical development issue, cooling technologies represent a challenge for climate change through refrigerant leakage and energy-related emissions. Cooling appliances, such as air conditioners or refrigerators, typically use refrigerants that damage the ozone layer and have a high global warming potential. In addition, cooling is energy-intensive, which can lead to major indirect carbon dioxide emissions. According to the IEA, energy demand solely from air conditioners – mainly driven by emerging economy cities – will increase threefold by 2050 (IEA, 2018[17]).

Yet, more cooling is called for if we want to meet the SDGs. This raises an important question: Is it possible to deliver "cooling for all" while meeting the climate objectives? Increased energy efficiency of cooling appliances or drastic greening of electricity grids alone will be insufficient. The implementation of the Kigali Agreement, which requires a major reduction of hydrofluorocarbons (HFCs) in the years to come, is expected to reduce the impact of cooling devices on global warming – and even more if these new appliances are energy efficient. However, this may not be sufficient to cancel out an increasingly growing number of appliances.

Solutions could become available when focusing on a needs-driven approach. For example, the cooling demand of buildings can be dramatically reduced using non-electric energies and temperature differentials such as waste heat, building efficient district cooling infrastructure into new city designs and solar energy that, in combination with new thermal storage solutions, can be used to power cooling equipment.

System-wide changes will require a careful assessment of country needs and circumstances to define scenarios and long-term pathways towards sustainable cooling for all. For example, governments can implement policies and regulations that improve building codes, rethink city planning, redesign food logistics and consumption chains and explore alternative materials and ways of producing and storing "cold energy".

Targeted policy action can help drive more sustainable city growth, particularly in land-use and transport policies. Examples include appropriately pricing car travel by reforming parking policies to better reflect the cost of providing parking, and introducing road pricing mechanisms. This should be accompanied by a shift towards greener urban transport, by investing in public and non-motorised transport infrastructure like bicycle lanes (OECD, 2018[4]).

Land-use policies can be reformed to encourage more sustainable urban development patterns. This includes relaxing maximum-density restrictions, shifting the cost of infrastructure provision to developers, streamlining land-use taxation to remove incentives for developing land on the outskirts of cities and introducing market-based instruments that encourage densification in key urban areas (OECD, 2018[4]). Urban planning can also encourage functionally and socially mixed neighbourhoods with access to green spaces (New Climate Economy, 2018[13]). Regulations governing how buildings are constructed can also play an important role in decarbonising cities (see Box 7.2).

For integrated planning, the appropriate scale of action is not necessarily contained within the administrative boundaries of cities, but rather the functional metropolitan area. Subnational and local governments need to strengthen collaboration between cities and different levels of governments, for example, by creating single entities with authority for transport and land use, and favouring more collaborative and co-ordinated forms of decision making. National and local transport agencies can develop joint pipelines of low-emission, resilient infrastructure projects aligned with long-term climate goals (see Chapter 2). Such projects should be selected on the basis of cost-benefit analysis with climate and resilience at their core.

7.2. Align national and local fiscal regulations with investment needs in cities

As urban populations grow, trillions of dollars will need to be spent on expanding and renewing urban infrastructure (OECD, 2014[18]). Much of this responsibility and expense falls on cities; on average, subnational governments account for 64% of climate-related spending and investment[1] (see Figure 7.1). However, this share ranges widely depending on the country context – for example, 98% of Japan's climate-related spending and investment falls to subnational governments, while in Iceland this accounts for 18%.

One of the primary challenges for cities in accessing sufficient financing is their limited ability to tax, which is typically constrained by legislation at higher levels of government. The Inter-American Development Bank (IDB) governance database shows that fewer than half of all countries have devolved fiscal or legislative powers to subnational governments (Floater et al., 2017[20]). Cities are further constrained in their ability to borrow; they may be limited by whether and how much they can borrow from the private sector (OECD, 2014[18]). According to the IDB database, 56% of countries do not allow borrowing of any kind by local governments (Floater et al., 2017[20]). Sometimes national frameworks also prevent cities from issuing bonds (see Box 7.3). While this feature may help to limit financial risks, it can also deprive cities of an important source of finance. Other financing mechanisms for climate-resilient urban infrastructure include the use of catastrophe bonds, the establishment of dedicated finance facilities, dedicated global climate funds, as well as official development assistance (ODA) for cities in developing countries.

Figure 7.1. **Subnational governments largely foot the bill for environment and climate investment**

Environmental and climate investment by level of government, selected OECD countries, 2000-2016

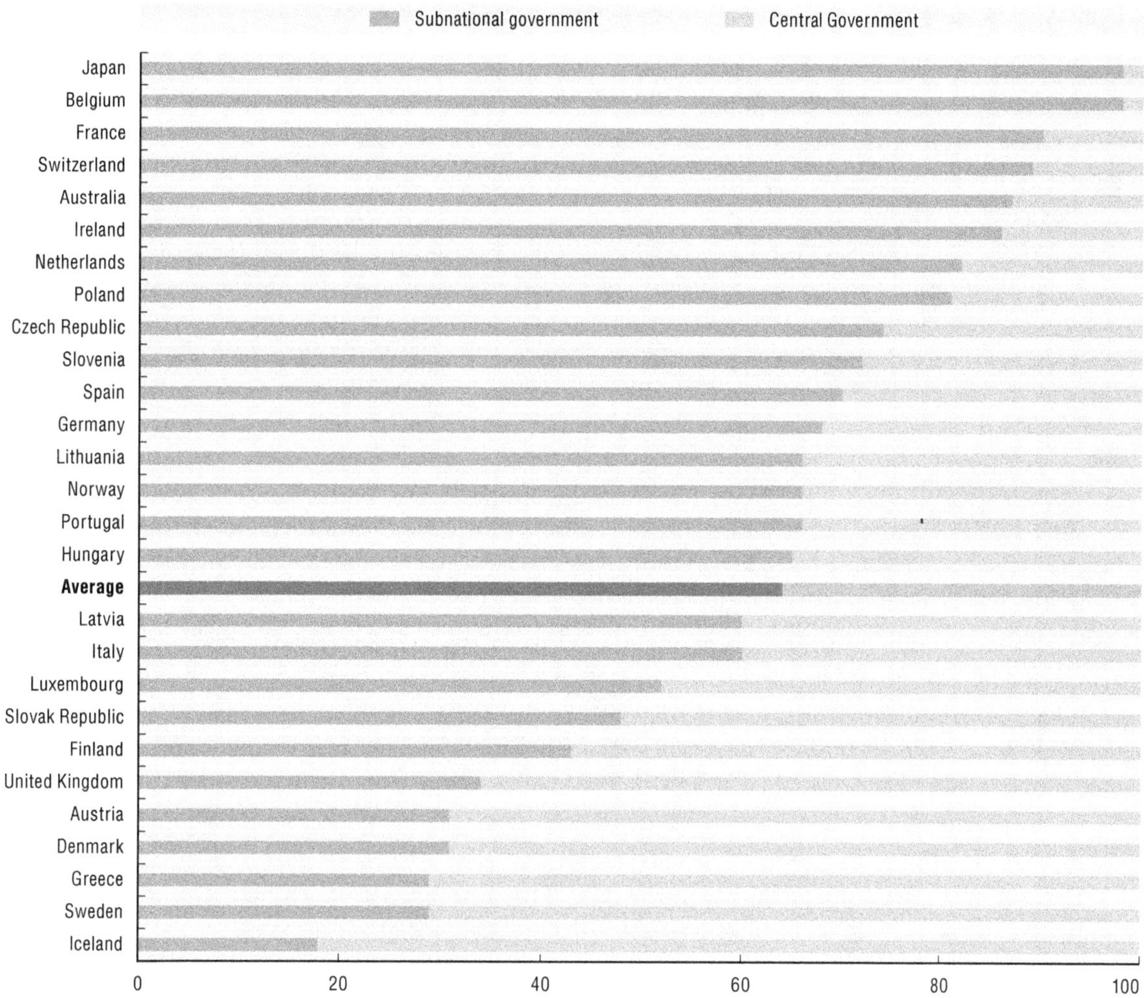

Note: Calculated by dividing total amount of subnational climate direct investment spending by the total amount of general government climate-related infrastructure investment, 2000-2016. Average represents the unweighted average of all countries presented in this graphic, rather than average for all OECD countries. Japan's spending data begins in 2005, Lithuania's in 2004, and Iceland's in 2013. Australia's spending data ends in 2015.

Source: OECD (2017[19]), "Government Expenditure by Function (COFOG)," OECD Statistics (database).

StatLink https://doi.org/10.1787/888933856492

Supportive national policy frameworks and legislation are necessary to ensure that cities have the resources, incentives and potential to implement effective climate initiatives. National policies and legislation typically determine what cities can do and the framework conditions within which they operate including, for example, their revenue-raising ability. A strong national framework using market-based instruments (e.g. carbon pricing, performance standards) can broaden the range of environmentally and economically effective options available to cities. National governments can also build environmental goals into national and urban planning strategies, and encourage climate action through grants and subsidies. It is equally important to identify national policies that conflict with or prevent local climate action.

Box 7.3. **The importance of green bonds for cities**

Financial instruments such as green bonds can provide an opportunity to raise funds for green infrastructure projects. The first green bonds for cities were issued in 2013. Since then, 180 bonds in 13 countries have been issued. For example, New York plans to use their green bond revenues on wastewater adaptation and a USD 1.7 billion subway expansion. Wuhan in central China has a total green bond issuance of USD 8.7 billion, with planned projects including flood protection and a public bicycle service.

Subnational green bond growth issuance is rising, and accounted for 21% of green bond issuance in 2017. Cities have begun to issue green bonds at record pace in order to help finance their infrastructure needs. However, before cities can issue bonds, they need national legislation to clearly articulate whether they can borrow and under what conditions, including from which institutions, how much, in what currencies and using what collateral.

Sources: Climate Bonds Initiative (2018[22]), *Green Bond Highlights 2017*; Climate Bonds Initiative (2017[23]), *Bonds and Climate Change: The State of the Market 2017*, *https://www.climatebonds.net/*

Cities with devolved revenue-raising capacity – such as Tokyo and Paris – can align their existing municipal revenue streams to help achieve climate goals (Slack, 2016[24]). For example, congestion charges and parking fees can help prompt users to use lower-emitting public transit alternatives, and property taxes and development charges can encourage density in urban areas (OECD, 2013[25]; OECD, 2018[4]). Some cities can also introduce emissions-pricing initiatives, offering the dual benefit of raising revenues that fund low-emission, resilient infrastructure while also helping to internalise the costs of emissions. For example, Beijing, Shenzhen and Tokyo have all implemented or are planning to implement emissions-trading schemes (World Bank and Ecofys, 2018[26]).

Municipalities in developing countries face the even greater challenge of having typically limited capacity or authority to raise revenues, but also the largest infrastructure deficits. Ensuring infrastructure resilience in the face of increasingly severe climate events will be key for the sustainability of cities (see Box 7.4). The financing gap is most evident in cities in low- and middle-income countries: Iwo (Nigeria), Lucena City (Philippines), and Pekalongan (Indonesia) raise only USD 14, USD 54, and USD 101 per resident per year, compared to Freiburg (Germany) and Bristol (United Kingdom), which have per capita budgets of USD 3 638 and USD 4 907 respectively (Löffler, 2016[27]).

Multi-national development banks and development finance institutions can provide technical support to facilitate access to international markets and propose city-specific financial instruments such as bonds and grants to scale up investment, and help improve credit-worthiness of cities through guarantee mechanisms. Coalitions such as the Cities Climate Finance Leadership Alliance, launched in 2014, work to mobilise and accelerate investment in low-emission, resilient infrastructure in cities and urban areas.

National finance ministries can help by reviewing the fiscal framework of cities and identifying misalignments with climate objectives, and by developing national legislation that clearly articulates whether cities can borrow and under what circumstances. Local governments can align local taxes and charges with low-emission, resilient development (such as introducing appropriately priced parking fees, congestion charges and emissions pricing), and reform fees and taxes that encourage sprawl.

Box 7.4. Improving cities' access to finance is essential for building urban resilience

In the coming decades, cities will have to grapple with increased demographic pressures and rapid urbanisation, while also adapting to new operating conditions for essential infrastructure and services due to climate change. The severity of the impacts of future climate events will depend on a range of factors, but high physical and economic costs can drastically hinder cities' ability to bounce back following a climate-related disaster (Goldstein, 2018[28]). This problem is even more complex in many developing countries, where cities' existing infrastructure stocks are insufficient, and must now be scaled up to provide services for burgeoning populations. In these countries, capital investment needs in infrastructure are huge, possibly in excess of USD 1 trillion per year. This recurring infrastructure deficit combined with strong population growth threatens the economic prospects of such cities, leading policy makers to explore new ways to pay for low-emission, resilient development. While climate action plans are emerging at the city level, funding and financing options available to local authorities, in both developing and advanced economies, can be limited due to creditworthiness concerns or national policy frameworks. However, some promising solutions exist.

From a management and system design perspective, some approaches can help system operators avoid or reduce the impacts of climate change on their systems, as presented hereafter:

- In the water sector, some municipalities are encouraging **'green' infrastructure projects** (e.g. parks that can act as short-term storm water retention ponds) instead of 'grey' (or manmade) systems that can be more costly to build and maintain.
- In the energy sector, **demand response schemes** that encourage households through differentiated pricing systems to consume less energy during peak demand periods have been set up by various utilities; and a **dedicated science team** was set up within the California-based Pacific Gas and Electricity company in 2016 to integrate the latest climate studies into the company's risk assessment process (PG&E, 2016[29]).

Cities are also starting to turn to a range of financing and regulatory approaches to support climate-resilient infrastructure investments. For example:

- **Land-use laws** and **building codes** can help manage citywide infrastructure needs by encouraging property owners to invest in climate-proofing as part of their building or landscaping design strategy.
- **Taxes with a dedicated climate focus** controlled by local authorities can support resilient infrastructure investments. While still a relatively new phenomenon, there are several examples from which lessons can be learned: for example, Mexico City offers a property tax reduction, averaging a 10% cut, to all new and existing building owners that install green roofs (C40, 2015[30]).
- **Public-Private Partnerships (PPPs)** can increase access to finance beyond what is available to governments, ensure cost containment, and help with timely delivery of climate-related projects. Moving forward, PPP contracts could include a "fitness for purpose" warranty that requires the private sector partner to ensure that the infrastructure delivers against its intended function over an extended timeframe. This implicitly forces the private party to account for climate change in their system design and operations.
- **Bilateral aid and ODA** are common sources of funding for energy, water and transport systems in most developing countries. Over the period 2010-12, an estimated USD 720 million per year, representing 8% of the total bilateral adaptation-related aid, was dedicated to climate-resilient infrastructure investments (OECD, 2014[31]; Ohshita and Johnson, 2017[32]). This number could be even higher if governments made this a priority as part of their request for support.
- **Dedicated global climate funds**, e.g. the Green Climate Fund, as well as green banks or facilities focusing solely on urban projects can help. While such green banks are mostly found in advanced economies, and the question of their capitalisation needs to be resolved, their narrow focus allows them to build in-house expertise quickly, meaning they can also to serve as a helpful technical resource to clients.

Box 7.4. **Improving cities' access to finance is essential for building urban resilience** *(cont.)*

Another promising development is the growing role of technical assistance initiatives aimed at facilitating cities' access to public and private finance for resilience projects. National governments again have a role to play here, as they create the essential operating conditions for their cities. While some governments may wish to keep a tight rein over these decisions, due to concerns about corruption or lack of internal capacity, a key question moving forward is whether and when national governments should revisit such restrictions, giving cities more room to manoeuvre on climate issues. At the 2017 One Planet Summit, the Global Covenant of Mayors called for "improved vertical policy alignments between national and local governments" for these very reasons. This will likely remain an ongoing concern, with financing implications, for cities and other local authorities engaged in climate resilience matters and planning.

Source: World Bank Group (2018[33]), Financing Resilient Urban Infrastructure: Lessons from World Bank and Global Experience (forthcoming), *Financing Climate Futures Case Studies.*

7.3. Build climate-related and project finance capacity in cities

In addition to the challenges facing local governments due to their weak fiscal autonomy, they also often lack capacity in areas such as measuring emissions, mainstreaming climate risks in infrastructure planning, and financing and delivering infrastructure projects efficiently. These capacity gaps not only impede governments' success in delivering on their climate objectives but also their borrowing ability.

Only 20% of the world's 150 largest cities have the basic analytical tools at their disposal for low-emission urban planning (World Bank, 2013[34]). Developing capacity in local governments and administrations is fundamental to make climate action work, particularly in developing countries that suffer from capacity constraints and severe vulnerabilities to the adverse effects of climate change. This is recognised in Article 11.2 of the Paris Agreement, which states that "[c]apacity-building should be country-driven, based on and responsive to national needs including at the national, subnational and local levels" (UNFCCC, 2015[35]).

Sufficient capacity can help bolster infrastructure investment, including a better understanding of administrative procedures, procurement procedures, co-ordination with other levels of government and across jurisdictions (see Box 7.5), and strategic planning. National governments can fund programmes that provide training and technical support to enhance access to private capital markets. Building institutional capacity and expertise can help cities prepare for and package infrastructure projects into attractive bankable projects for private investors. Cities could also strengthen their long-term planning capacity (see Chapter 2), including their use of tools such as cost-benefit analysis, to ensure a strong information base is being used for decision making.

National governments and development finance institutions can help by building local capacity to access private capital markets and to work with the private sector (OECD, 2014[18]). They can strengthen capacities and skills in developing risk-informed urban plans, and in designing and selecting urban infrastructure that takes into account a range of future climate conditions and the associated uncertainties. They can also help build climate-related capacities to develop long-term low-emission strategies and measure greenhouse gas emissions and progress.

Assisting cities through strengthened financial performance and enhancing city leaders' knowledge of revenue management, expenditure control, debt management, asset maintenance and capital investment planning is central to unlocking and improving creditworthiness (World Bank, 2018[37]). Creditworthiness can be affected by the inability to collect revenue, which limits a city's capacity to borrow. The lack of transparent accounting practices is another important barrier, particularly in developing countries.

Box 7.5. **Kommuninvest**

Kommuninvest is a co-operative organisation of Swedish municipalities that work together to bring down the cost of loans. It began in the 1980s and today accounts for over 40% of Swedish local government borrowing. It helps build credit for cities in order to facilitate investment. All members must accept liability for Kommuninvest's obligations.

There have never been any credit losses since the entity's inception and it is the only company in Sweden that has the highest credit rating from Moody's and Standard & Poor's. Canada, France, New Zealand and the United Kingdom are building on Kommuninvest's model for similar operations.

Source: Kommuninvest (2018[36]), "Our vision", Kommuninvest website, *https://kommuninvest.se/en/about-us-3/vision-and-basic-concept/*

Estimates suggest that less than 4% of the largest 500 cities in developing countries are considered creditworthy in international markets, and less than 20% are considered creditworthy in local markets (World Bank, 2013[38]). Improving creditworthiness can have tremendous impacts: just USD 1 of investment in improving city creditworthiness in a developing country can leverage more than USD 100 in private investment in sustainable urban infrastructure (World Bank, 2013[38]). City creditworthiness initiatives and project preparation facilities, such as the World Bank's City Resilience Program (CRP) and the C40 Finance Facility, can support public entities' capacities in developing bankable projects and scale up their investment in infrastructure. This applies in particular to cities in developing countries, as the majority still lack access to external financing sources.

Strong leadership among local elected representatives can increase the ambition of climate and inclusive growth measures undertaken by cities. In recognition of the key role of cities in tackling inequalities, the OECD created a global coalition of Champion Mayors for Inclusive Growth in March 2016, which put forward four priority policies: education, labour markets, housing and the urban environment, and infrastructure and public services. The coalition's agenda includes diagnosing policy misalignments affecting climate action, developing evidence on the benefits and potential regressive impacts of climate action on inclusive growth, facilitating best practice sharing, as well as identifying bottlenecks to entrepreneurship. This coalition provides the leadership that is often missing at a city level to ensure that cities plan and finance low-emission, resilient infrastructure to ensure a sustainable and fair local economy (OECD, 2015[39]).

7.4. Seize the development benefits of low-emission, resilient planning

Income inequality is already higher in cities than their national averages – and likely to be worsened by climate change (Hallegatte et al., 2016[10]; OECD, 2018[14]). Cities therefore have a crucial role to play in implementing and delivering the low-emission transition in an inclusive way. The health implications of poverty in cities are already startling: while the richest 40% of urban dwellers are likely to reach the age of 70 or more, the poorest 20% struggle to reach 55 years (UN-Habitat, 2015[40]). In Baltimore (US) and London (UK), life expectancy can vary by 20 years across neighbourhoods (OECD, 2016[41]). Globally, nearly one billion people live in slum-like conditions, many of which are extremely vulnerable to climate impacts (UN-Habitat, 2016[2]).

Core climate policies – such as those relating to energy, transport and carbon taxation; subsidy and pricing reforms; support for renewable and low-carbon energy; energy efficiency programmes; and transport planning and management – have the potential to affect household spending and the affordability of energy, transport services and housing. Policies outside the climate portfolio can also influence climate and inclusive growth. For instance, local tax policies, by affecting the costs and benefits of land use, can have a significant impact on emissions and housing affordability. Considering the impacts of policies at the subnational level on development and inclusiveness is therefore central to strategic, cohesive planning (see Box 7.6).

Box 7.6. **OECD Framework on Inclusive Growth**

Climate change, globalisation, digitalisation and demographic changes are transforming the way economies work, providing new opportunities for growth, but also raising the risk of deeper inequalities if the gains from growth are not evenly shared among people, firms and regions. The OECD Inclusive Growth Initiative puts the emphasis on policies that can improve the perspectives of the bottom 40% of the income distribution:

1. **Invest in people and places that have been left behind** through: (i) targeted quality childcare, early education and life-long acquisition of skills; (ii) effective access to quality healthcare, justice, housing, infrastructures; and (iii) optimal natural resource management for sustainable growth.
2. **Support business dynamism and inclusive labour markets** through: (i) broad-based innovation and technology diffusion; (ii) strong competition and vibrant entrepreneurship; (iii) access to good quality jobs, especially for women and underrepresented groups; and (iv) enhanced resilience and adaptation to the future of work.
3. **Build efficient and responsive governments** through: (i) aligned policy packages across the whole of government; (ii) integration of distributional aspects upfront in the design of policy; and (iii) assessing policies for their impact on inclusiveness and growth.

Source: OECD (2018[42]), *Opportunities for All: A Framework for Policy Action on Inclusive Growth.*

Climate policies and strategies present both threats and opportunities for more inclusive growth. If appropriately planned, low-emission, resilient infrastructure can have positive impacts on vulnerable populations; for instance, increased investment in urban transport systems generally improves access to jobs for low-income populations.

However, such investments can also lead to counterproductive knock-on effects in the long run. Upgrading the public transport system may in some cases lead to gentrification and the displacement of lower income groups to lower quality, job-poor neighbourhoods, thereby reducing their access to jobs and services (ITF, 2017[43]). In the absence of redistribution mechanisms, carbon pricing may disproportionately affect low-income people. Another example is congestion charges, which tend to be regressive and, in the absence of compensating policies, risk disproportionately affecting low-income households living in the urban periphery where housing prices are cheaper. However, if the revenues of congestion charges are used to provide an affordable and reliable alternative (public transport), they can generate more equitable outcomes (ITF, 2017[43]). Focusing on housing quality and affordability can improve the productivity of home-based workers who comprise a significant proportion of the work force in Asia (14% in India), and the vast majority of whom are women (Chen and Sinha, 2016[44]).

While the transition to a low-emission economy will yield benefits in certain economic sectors, it will also reduce jobs for workers in emissions-intensive sectors. Low-skilled workers are likely to be most significantly affected, while medium- and high-skilled workers will be largely shielded and are also more likely to benefit from opportunities in green technology and innovation. These impacts can be limited – and a high level of employment and a fair distribution of transition costs maintained – if governments can put effective policies in place to prepare the labour markets. Specifically, governments can focus on supply-side policies, with active labour market policies and skill development systems that can help facilitate a smooth reintegration of workers into employment. Demand-side policies can foster a competitive green sector through strong product market competition and moderate employment protection. Finally, income support, such as unemployment insurance and in-work benefits, can ensure a fairer transition for workers (OECD, 2018[14]).

Subnational and local governments can help by mainstreaming inclusiveness in infrastructure planning (see Box 7.7). Cities can also integrate climate and inclusiveness outcomes by investing the revenues from environmental taxes and fees in measures that boost inclusive growth. They can take advantage of skills development and job-creation opportunities in urban infrastructure financing and investment, particularly relating to energy efficiency investments, and explore the potential for green bonds to achieve both climate and inclusion goals.

Box 7. 7. **Strengthen capacity to track subnational data on climate spending and investment**

Many subnational governments have set climate targets and are incorporating climate change adaptation and mitigation into their budget priorities. However, climate-related spending and investment at the local level remain insufficient. Between 2000 and 2016, climate-related investments grew by only 0.5% annually (in real terms on average), compared to 2.6% for central governments. Comparing the levels and trends of such investments is currently not possible across subnational governments due to lack of consistent data. This in turn makes it difficult to evaluate progress towards the Paris Agreement in a standardised way, and to adjust climate action at the subnational level accordingly. Thus, there is a need to address the institutional, human and data capacity gaps that currently lower the quality and quantity of data for tracking local climate-related spending and investments.

Few countries have developed climate-specific statistics, and many use other categories of national accounts to capture climate-related spending and investments (e.g. counting energy efficiency investments in hospitals under health-related functions). Some countries have developed approaches to tracking climate expenditures at the national level (e.g. Belgium, France and Germany), but they all use different categories and classification systems. Other countries' systems provide incomplete data models. Only three European countries produce complete national data on mitigation spending, and none maintain comprehensive data on adaptation spending. These issues are even more obvious at the subnational level, especially for non-OECD countries (including some members of the G20).

To ensure cities have the adequate data, capacities and instruments to deliver the scale and speed of the transformation needed, governments should strengthen data collection, statistical systems and methodological approaches to track progress on climate objectives. This could be done in co-ordination with international fora such as the G20, and with the support of the OECD and other international organisations, building on preliminary efforts to track and compare existing subnational climate-related spending and investments.

Source: OECD (2018[11]), Financing climate objectives in cities and regions to deliver sustainable and inclusive growth (forthcoming), *Financing Climate Futures Case Studies.*

Some cities are already incorporating such explicit equity dimensions into their climate strategies. For example, New York's 'OneNYC' roadmap aims to make the city not only more dynamic economically, but also more just, sustainable and resilient. It includes environmental targets (such as fully eliminating waste going to landfills), steps for adaptation (such as strengthening coastal defences against flooding and sea rise) and equity measures (including lifting 800 000 New Yorkers out of poverty by 2025, setting the minimum wage at USD 15 and implementing education and retraining initiatives) (New York City, 2013[45]).

Another example is Seoul's Energy Welfare Public Private Partnership Programme. It aims to address energy poverty in Seoul, which affects over 10% of households, by increasing their energy independence through efficiency home upgrades for example. It also provides training to allow disadvantaged job seekers to become energy efficiency consultants for low-income households. The programme is funded by public and private sources, including monetary savings earned through demand-side management measures, among other elements (OECD, 2018[14]).

Notes

1. Climate investments can be defined as the acquisition (including purchases of new or second-hand assets) of assets for climate purposes (e.g. installing coastal defences against flooding and sea level rise). Climate spending can be defined as the amount of money spent on operating and maintaining these (e.g. strengthening coastal defences).

References

C40 (2015), "Green Building City Market Briefs: Mexico City", in *Green Building City Market Briefs*, C40, *https://www.c40.org/researches/c40-usgbc-and-wgbc-green-building-city-market-brief-compendium* (accessed on 22 October 2018). [30]

Chen, M. and S. Sinha (2016), "Home-based workers and cities", *Environment and Urbanization*, Vol. 28/2, pp. 343-358, *http://dx.doi.org/10.1177/0956247816649865*. [44]

Climate Bonds Initiative (2017), *Bonds and Climate Change: The State of the Market 2017*, Climate Bonds Initiative, *https://www.climatebonds.net/files/reports/cbi-sotm_2017-bondsclimatechange.pdf* (accessed on 27 September 2018). [23]

Climate Bonds Initiative (2018), *Green Bond Highlights 2017*, *https://www.climatebonds.net/files/reports/cbi-green-bonds-highlights-2017.pdf* (accessed on 24 July 2018). [22]

Floater, G. et al. (2017), "Global Review of Finance for Sustainable Urban Infrastructure", Coalition for Urban Transitions, *http://newclimateeconomy.net/content/cities-working-papers*. (accessed on 24 July 2018). [20]

Goldstein, M. (2018), "Puerto Rico's Positive Business Slogans Can't Keep the Lights On", *The New York Times*, *https://www.nytimes.com/2018/03/05/business/puerto-rico-business-maria.html* (accessed on 22 October 2018). [28]

Gouldson, A. et al. (2018), "The Economic and Social Benefits of Low-Carbon Cities: A Systematic Review of the Evidence", Coalition for Urban Transitions, London and Washington, DC, *http://newclimateeconomy.net/content/cities-working-papers*. (accessed on 22 October 2018). [15]

Hallegatte, S. et al. (2013), "Future flood losses in major coastal cities", *Nature Climate Change*, Vol. 3/9, pp. 802-806, *http://dx.doi.org/10.1038/nclimate1979*. [9]

Hallegatte, S. et al. (2016), *Shock Waves: Climate Change and Development Series Managing the Impacts of Climate Change on Poverty*, The World Bank, Washington, DC, *https://openknowledge.worldbank.org/bitstream/handle/10986/22787/9781464806735.pdf* (accessed on 27 September 2018). [10]

IEA (2018), *The Future of Cooling: Opportunities for energy-efficient air conditioning*, International Energy Agency, Paris, *https://www.iea.org/publications/freepublications/publication/The_Future_of_Cooling.pdf* (accessed on 26 October 2018). [17]

INRIX (2017), *INRIX Global Traffic Scorecard 2017*, INRIX, *http://inrix.com/scorecard/* (accessed on 22 October 2018). [6]

ITF (2017), *Income Inequality, Social Inclusion and Mobility*, OECD Publishing, Paris, *https://www.itf-oecd.org/income-inequality-social-inclusion-mobility* (accessed on 22 October 2018). [43]

ITF (2017), *ITF Transport Outlook 2017*, OECD Publishing, Paris, *http://dx.doi.org/10.1787/9789282108000-en*. [5]

Kommuninvest (2018), *Our vision*, Kommuninvest Web Portal, *https://kommuninvest.se/en/about-us-3/vision-and-basic-concept/* (accessed on 22 October 2018). [36]

Löffler, G. (2016), "Analysis of the State of Local Finance in Intermediary Cities", United Cities and Local Governments (UCLG), *https://www.gold.uclg.org/sites/default/files/Loffler_EN.pdf#overlay-context=reports/other/gold-report-iv* (accessed on 25 July 2018). [27]

New Climate Economy (2014), *Better Growth, Better Climate*, New Climate Economy, Washington, DC, *https://newclimateeconomy.report/2014/*. [12]

New Climate Economy (2018), *Unlocking the Inclusive Growth Story of the 21st Century*, New Climate Economy, Washington, DC, *https://newclimateeconomy.report/2018/*. [13]

New York City (2013), *One New York: The Plan for a Strong and Just City*, *http://www.nyc.gov/html/onenyc/downloads/pdf/publications/OneNYC.pdf* (accessed on 22 October 2018). [45]

OECD (2010), *Cities and Climate Change*, OECD Publishing, Paris, *http://dx.doi.org/10.1787/9789264091375-en*. [3]

OECD (2014), *Cities and Climate Change: National governments enabling local action*, OECD Publishing, Paris, *https://www.oecd.org/env/cc/Cities-and-climate-change-2014-Policy-Perspectives-Final-web.pdf* (accessed on 22 October 2018). [18]

OECD (2014), *OECD DAC Statistics: Aid to Urban Climate Change Adaptation*, OECD Publishing, Paris, *https://www.oecd.org/dac/environment-development/Urban%20Adaptation%20Flyer.pdf* (accessed on 22 October 2018). [31]

OECD (2015), *All on Board: Making Inclusive Growth Happen*, OECD Publishing, Paris, *http://dx.doi.org/10.1787/9789264218512-en*. [39]

OECD (2016), *Making Cities Work for All: Data and Actions for Inclusive Growth*, OECD Publishing, Paris, *http://dx.doi.org/10.1787/9789264263260-en*. [41]

OECD (2016), *The Economic Consequences of Outdoor Air Pollution*, OECD Publishing, Paris, *http://dx.doi.org/10.1787/9789264257474-en*. [7]

OECD (2017), *Government expenditure by function (COFOG)*, OECD Statistics (database), *https://stats.oecd.org/Index.aspx?DataSetCode=SNA_TABLE11* (accessed on 22 October 2018). [19]

OECD (2018), "Financing climate objectives in cities and regions to deliver sustainable and inclusive growth (forthcoming)", *Financing Climate Futures Case Studies*, OECD Publishing, Paris. [11]

OECD (2018), *Inclusive Growth in Seoul, Korea*, OECD Publishing, Paris, *http://dx.doi.org/10.1787/9789264290198-en*. [14]

OECD (2018), *Opportunities for All: A Framework for Policy Action on Inclusive Growth*, OECD Publishing, Paris, *http://dx.doi.org/10.1787/9789264301665-en*. [42]

OECD (2018), *Rethinking Urban Sprawl: Moving Towards Sustainable Cities*, OECD Publishing, Paris, *http://dx.doi.org/10.1787/9789264189881-en*. [4]

Ohshita, S. and K. Johnson (2017), *Resilient urban energy: making city systems energy efficient, low carbon, and resilient in a changing climate*, European Council for an Energy Efficient Economy, *https://www.eceee.org/library/conference_proceedings/eceee_Summer_Studies/2017/3-local-action/resilient-urban-energy-making-city-systems-energy-efficient-low-carbon-and-resilient-in-a-changing-climate/* (accessed on 22 October 2018). [32]

PG&E (2016), *Climate Change Vulnerability Assessment*, Pacific Gas and Electricity Company (PG&E), *http://www.pgecurrents.com/wp-content/uploads/2016/02/PGE_climate_resilience.pdf*. [29]

SE4All (2018), *Chilling Prospects: Providing Sustainable Cooling for All*, Sustainable Energy for All (SE4All), *https://www.seforall.org/sites/default/files/SEforALL_CoolingForAll-Report.pdf* (accessed on 26 October 2018). [16]

UNDESA (2015), "Risks of Exposure and Vulnerability to Natural Disasters at the City Level: A Global Overview", *https://esa.un.org/Unpd/Wup/Publications/Files/WUP2014-TechnicalPaper-NaturalDisaster.pdf* (accessed on 25 July 2018). [8]

UNDESA (2018), *World Urbanization Prospects: The 2018 Revision*, United Nations Department of Economic and Social Affairs, New York City, *https://esa.un.org/unpd/wup/Publications/Files/WUP2018-KeyFacts.pdf* (accessed on 22 October 2018). [1]

UNFCCC (2015), *Paris Agreement*, *https://unfccc.int/sites/default/files/english_paris_agreement.pdf* (accessed on 03 July 2018). [35]

UN-Habitat (2015), "Informal Settlements", *Habitat III Issue Papers*, No. 22, United Nations Human Settlements Programme, New York City, *https://unhabitat.org/wp-content/uploads/2015/04/Habitat-III-Issue-Paper-22_Informal-Settlements.pdf* (accessed on 22 October 2018). [40]

UN-Habitat (2016), *Urbanization and Development: Emerging Futures*, United National Human Settlements Programme (UN-Habitat), Nairobi, *https://www.unhabitat.org/wp-content/uploads/2014/03/WCR-%20Full-Report-2016.pdf* (accessed on 27 September 2018). [2]

World Bank (2013), *Financing Sustainable Cities: How We're Helping Africa's Cities Raise Their Credit Ratings*, World Bank Web Portal, *http://www.worldbank.org/en/news/feature/2013/10/24/financing-sustainable-cities-africa-creditworthy* (accessed on 22 October 2018). [38]

World Bank (2013), *Planning and Financing Low-Carbon, Livable Cities*, World Bank Web Portal, *http://www.worldbank.org/en/news/feature/2013/09/25/planning-financing-low-carbon-cities* (accessed on 22 October 2018). [34]

World Bank (2018), *City Creditworthiness Initiative: A Partnership to Deliver Municipal Finance*, World Bank Web Portal, *http://www.worldbank.org/en/topic/urbandevelopment/brief/city-creditworthiness-initiative* (accessed on 22 October 2018). [37]

World Bank and Ecofys (2018), *State and Trends of Carbon Pricing 2018*, World Bank, Washington, DC, *https://openknowledge.worldbank.org/handle/10986/29687*. [26]

World Bank Group (2018), "Financing Resilient Urban Infrastructure: Lessons from World Bank and Global Experience (forthcoming)", *Financing Climate Futures Case Studies*, World Bank Group, Washington, DC. [33]

OECD PUBLISHING, 2, rue André-Pascal, 75775 PARIS CEDEX 16
(97 2018 46 1 P) ISBN 978-92-64-30810-7 – 2018

www.ingramcontent.com/pod-product-compliance
Lightning Source LLC
Chambersburg PA
CBHW061219240926
51846CB00006B/1281
9789264308107